FAIRACRES PUBL

# Cosmos, Crisis & Christ

## Essays of
## Wendy Robinson

### Collected & Edited by
### Andrew Louth

© 2024 SLG Press
First Edition 2024

Fairacres Publications No. 211

Print ISBN 978-0-7283-0373-7
Fairacres Publications Series ISSN 0307-1405

Edited and typeset in Palatino Linotype by Julia Craig-McFeely

Biblical quotations are taken from the New Revised Standard Version of the Bible unless otherwise noted

SLG Press
Convent of the Incarnation
Fairacres • Oxford
www.slgpress.co.uk


Printed by
Grosvenor Group Ltd, Loughton, Essex

# CONTENTS

# ACKNOWLEDGEMENTS

I would like to acknowledge the help given by those I consulted, at various stages, about this project. They include, first of all, Katharine Hall and Rowan Williams, as well as Hilary Robinson, Gregory Bridge, Chris O'Neill, Andrew Teal, Nancy Forest-Flier, Mary Cunningham, Sarah Coakley, and finally Julia Craig-McFeely, who saw it all through the Press and much improved it. I am grateful, too, to the Sisters of the Love of God, and their enthusiasm for the book and for their suggestions.

ANDREW LOUTH

Previously-published essays by Wendy Robinson are presented here in new editions with minor corrections and some editorial notes rather than being reproduced exactly as they appeared in their original form. Every effort has been made to seek reproduction permission for all of these essays, but in several cases the organizations who originally published them no longer exist. We apologize for any unintended infringement that may therefore occur.

Lines from *The Sleeping Lord* by David Jones are quoted with permission from Faber & Faber Limited.

*A Journey to the Russian Orthodox Church: An Ecumenical Journey to Orthodoxy*, first published in 2007 in the series 'Servants of Christ the King Pamplets'.

'The Quest for the Heart of the Work: An Ontological Approach to Spirituality and Psychotherapy/Counselling', first published in *Psychodynamic Counselling* 4/3 (August 1998).

*The Lost Traveller's Dream: Developing a Theology for Working with Mental Illness*, first published in 1995 as a pamphlet by Oxford Christian Institute for Counselling.

'Sounding Stones: Reflections on the Mystery of the Feminine', first published in *Fairacres Chronicle*, Summer 1984, Vol. 17, No. 2, then as Fairacres Publications No. 99 (SLG Press, 1987).

*Exploring Silence*, first published by SLG Press in 1974 as Fairacres Publications No. 36, then in 2013 in a revised edition as Fairacres Publications No. 170; Illustration: Militza Zernov, *Icon of the 'Perfect' Silence*, property of the author.

*Mary, The Flower and Fruit of Worship: The Mother of God in the Orthodox Tradition*, first published in *Abba: The Tradition of Orthodoxy in the West. Festschrift for Bishop Kallistos Ware*, ed. John Behr, Andrew Louth, Dimitri Conomos. Reproduced by kind permission of the editors.

'Anger', unpublished retreat address to SLG Oblates at the Convent of the Incarnation, Fairacres, March 1988. Reproduced by kind permission of the Sisters of the Love of God, Convent of the Incarnation, Fairacres, Oxford.

# ESSAYS OF
# WENDY
# ROBINSON

# A Journey to the Russian Orthodox Church: An Ecumenical Journey to Orthodoxy

## Introduction

I want to talk about Orthodox Spirituality but it seems to me that I must say something first about where I am coming from. You will realize that I am a walking ecumenical movement. There have been significant changes within my life, in which there has been some underlying unity, which I hope at best is God-given. I want to know how this will resonate with your experiences—whether you will agree or disagree. Conversation about these things is what sometimes seems to me to matter most.

I am reminded of a story about my 4-year old granddaughter, Iona. When she was four, she came to me and said, 'Grannie, I know what "agree" means, but what does "disagree" mean?' She loves words. Grannie tried to explain. 'I see,' she said, 'It is when I am right and you are wrong.'

'How does it feel when that happens,' asked Grannie, playing for time. 'Well, I am happy because I am right. You are unhappy, because you are wrong.' 'Would you like Grannie to go on being unhappy?' Unexpectedly she came back half-an-hour later and added, 'If you would agree that I am right, then you could be happy too!'

Do we ever change?

Conversation on these matters, as Archbishop Rowan never ceases to emphasize, is our one ongoing hope. It needs teamwork. I use that word because it reminds me of my grandson, Iona's brother, a year younger than her. He rushed up to me recently to say that they were doing teamwork. 'It is very important, Grannie. We are doing TEAMWORK'. He ran back to where they were playing. Less than ten seconds later he had hit his sister on the head with a little wooden hammer, which 'I just happened to have in my hand, Grannie'. I hope we can do better this weekend!

I was brought up on a sheep farm in the Yorkshire Dales with a lot of mystical experience of transcendence and a sense of presence on those grand moors. There was a reciprocal invocation between the Spirit and the 'Spirit-in-the-wind' which always blew. My identification with Emily Brontë went deep. Fortunately I never found a Heathcliff! When

I went West to university in Bristol, with all the softening of scenery and climate that was quite difficult to tangle with at first; me with my Pennine backbone and my three adjectives—Good, Bad, and Nobbut middlin. The speech seemed so flowery.

One day there happened one of those significant coincidences. I set off to the poetry society—and found myself hemmed into a crowded room. I did not realize that poetry was so popular. That was until a discovered that I was in a 'squash' meeting of a University mission. Out of that came an experience of the living Christ and the commitment of my life to him. I never regret that experience of committed evangelicalism. It taught me to read the Bible and to pray, and to go on believing that Christ is 'able to keep that which I have committed unto Him.' (2 Tim. 1:12).

But I went on to teach young delinquent girls (14–18) in an Approved School and suddenly the language world of evangelical faith no longer seemed to touch the experiences I was having. My middle-class values were turned upside down. And it was then that contacts with Quakers at university were salvific. With the Society of Friends I found a faith language that included profound social thinking. I became an anti-nuclear marcher and demonstrator for political freedoms, end-of-Empire stuff, and I also began to find the meaning of silence in worship and prayer, which fitted in with the moors and has remained a constant binding feature of experience ever since—one of my bonds with the Servants of Christ the King.

In my job I found real corruption in some of the authority figures and began the uneasy task of trying to learn how to 'speak truth to power', and how to try to remain sane under pressure: Quaker friends were an invaluable support. I became a psychiatric social worker in self-defence, and worked in a large psychiatric hospital, trying to learn that institutions will go on long after we are dead, and that reforming zeal needs to find a small focus and throw energy into working at that, and not thinking one can change everything.

Another set of coincidences sent me out for a change to work in Botswana (still a Protectorate then) in Serowe where Seretse and Ruth

Khama were living. I there encountered the Kalahari desert and a scene of bleak 'transcendence' very different form the moors of my childhood. I began to glimpse what the sacraments might be about, as mediators between the Transcendent and Us—and back to Christ and the meaning of the Incarnation.

I went out, twelve days to Capetown, on the *Windsor Castle*, Union Castle Line and on board I met a man with a copy of Jung's *Modern Man in Search of a Soul* under his arm. And the book under my arm was John Robinson's *Honest to God*. It was much later that the man revealed himself as John Robinson's brother, Edward.

I became ill in Botswana and at Edward's invitation went up to Salisbury for a Christmas break. There I met—aha! the plot thickens—Fr Gonville ffrench-Beytagh—who from then on had a great effect on my (on our) life. I came back into a sacramental Church. I went on learning about Life, Prayer, God, from that dear and beloved man, who was without doubt the finest pastoral priest I have ever met.

Edward was in his early forties and was exercised whether he could take on marriage that should last forever. When asked, Gonville replied: 'It isn't for ever, Edward. It's only for life!' For some reason this shifted the problem and we married.

After some racy and distinctively helpful compressed preparations with Gonville, Edward went back to finish things off in Rhodesia (Zambia) where he was working, as I, to finish off my work in Botswana. As evidence of Gonville's pastoral genius I wrote him a long letter, confessional, from Botswana. The post was very unreliable. He immediately sent a telegram to say, 'Marvellous letter received. Letter following'.

My early links with the Servants of Christ the King were through Gonville and Alison. I have always used your 'method' in group work I have done, religious or secular.[1] It has been a marvellous resource. Gonville introduced me to contemplative prayer and to the idea of the religious life, which, he always teased—I was lucky to meet only after

---

[1] For an introduction to the SCK 'method', see Brian (Gregory) Bridge, *Waiting on God: Seeking God's Calling Together in Small Groups* (Cambridge: Grove Books, 2013).

I had married. He also introduced me to the Jesus Prayer.[2] That in turn led me to contact with the Orthodox Church, when we moved to Oxford (three sons later and Edward beginning work with the Religious Experience Research Unit in Oxford).

I became Orthodox in 1980. It has been right for me: the length and depth of its worship, its rich symbolism, its teaching of the way of silence and stillness in prayer gets underneath all that I do in my work as a psychotherapist—with symptoms, nightmares, deep personal journeyings.

My life—personal and professional—has always been lived with a creative and sometimes taxing tension between the worlds of depth psychology and my religious faith. I will end with a story from our earlier family life with our sons. We were once on a wet Welsh holiday. You know the kind. We had lunch in a pub. A family fracas broke out. In ringing tones one son declared, 'The trouble with this family is that my father thinks he knows everything and my mother thinks she understands everything. My trouble is my mother understands me. She's a psychotherapist, you see.'

Oh to be so misunderstood! How we need that sometimes!

After such a vast personal diversion, which I hope you will forgive and will share some of your journeyings in response, I now turn more directly to Orthodox Spirituality.

## *Orthodox Spirituality*

If you want to understand Orthodoxy, the Orthodox will always tell you: 'Come and see'. You can't learn it from reading. It is the experience of Orthodox worship that will reveal what it is. What it does is what it is. The worship is rich, long, deeply symbolic, cumulative in its effects and with a lot of liturgical movement, incense, chanting…

---

[2] 'Lord Jesus Christ, Son of the living God, have mercy on me, a sinner' [This is the form of the prayer as Wendy cites it. More common is the form: 'Lord Jesus Christ, Son of God, have mercy on me, a sinner'. Wendy's version assimilates the traditional form to Peter's confession of Christ, cf. Matt. 16:16. Ed.]

The chanting—each country has a different musical tradition and sound. Perhaps one could speak of the 'heart music' of Russia and the 'gut chanting' of Greece—but that would oversimplify. The Orthodox tradition of worship and prayer, held in the depth of the monastic life, is wonderful. But its ethnic politics stinks, even when historically understandable. Politics is still conducted with poisonous rancour. So, judge not that we be not judged, let us concentrate on the essentials. Here is the story of the conversion of Russia.

Prince Vladimir sent out envoys to see which religion his country should adopt. They returned to Kiev and told him of an Orthodox liturgy which they had attended in Constantinople, in the Great Church of Hagia Sophia. They said,

> We knew not whether we were in heaven or on earth. For on earth there is no such splendour or such beauty and we are a loss to know how to describe it. We only know that God dwells there amongst men... for we cannot forget that beauty.[3]

My godmother in Orthodoxy was Militza Zernova, wife of Nicolas Zernov, whom some of you may have met. They were refugees from Russia in the 1922 purge and part of the 'Russian Religious Renaissance' in Paris in the 20s and 30s. They were also indefatigable workers in this country teaching and organizing conferences, usually ecumenical, to help us to understand Orthodoxy. Militza always emphasized the importance of antinomies,[4] that the faith could only be expressed through

---

[3] *The Russian Primary Chronicle: The Laurentian Text*, trans. and ed. by Samuel Hazzard Cross and Olgerd P. Sherbowitz-Wetzor (Cambridge MA: The Mediaeval Academy of America, 1953), 111.

[4] Antinomy—a contradiction between two conclusions that are themselves reasonable. [Or more precisely, rationally demonstrable. Originally a legal term for opposing judgments that can be legally justified. Used by Immanuel Kant as a key term in his philosophy, picked up by Fr Pavel Florensky (1882–1937), mentor to Fr Sergii Bulgakov (1871–1944), to whom the Zernovs were close. A key term in the philosophical vocabulary of many thinkers of the 'Russian Religious Renaissance': more or less the equivalent of 'paradox'. Ed.]

profound opposites which have to be held in tension—creative, life-giving, sometimes crucifying in their intensity.

Here is a passage from the writings of Fr Lev Gillet expressing some of those antinomies. He was wise, witty, and intense, small in stature but great in wisdom; a French monk and a convert, who lived and worked at St Basil's House in London. He actually died on the day I was received in 1980.[5]

> O strange Orthodox Church, so poor and so weak… maintained as if by a miracle through so many vicissitudes and struggles; Church of contrasts, so traditional and yet at the same time so free, so archaic and yet so alive, so ritualistic and yet so personally mystical; Church where the Evangelical pearl of great price is preciously safeguarded— yet often beneath a layer of dust. Church which has so frequently proved incapable of action, yet which knows as does no other, how to sing the joy of Pascha.[6]

Both (opposites) are so true.

As Paul Evdokimov says—the opposite of Sin is not Virtue, but the Faith of the Saints. What we need to do is to immerse ourselves humbly and with true repentance in the new life of Christ into which the Spirit can lead us. In each liturgy there is a spiritual life—humility, able sometimes to find the gift of the Spirit which is the gift of tears over our constant choosing of death and destructive ways of living, choosing death rather than life—a new life in Christ. There is a particular emphasis in the Russian Orthodox tradition on what they call in Slavonic *umilenie*—tender loving compassion in all humility and acknowledgment of what makes us truly lovingly human together.

The shape of traditional Orthodox churches, not Gothic but domed, perhaps nearer to the early Romanesque than our style in the

---

[5] [29 March, Lazarus Saturday (the day before Palm Sunday) in the Orthodox Calendar that year. Ed.]

[6] From a homily given at a memorial service for the death of his friend, Archimandrite Irénée Winnaert, in February 1938: quoted by Elisabeth Behr-Sigel in *Un Moine de l'Église d'Orient: le père Lev Gillet* (Paris: Éditions du Cerf, 1993), 173.

West, helps the spirit, too: rounded, earthed, like the Spirit hovering and brooding over the deeps of the cosmos and of human beings—the abyss of our being called out to the abyss of God's love. In the church, there are no pews, so one cannot become pew-bound! There may be a few chairs for those who need them. More movement is possible for people around the icons, or in and out with children. This may explain why parents with children feel accepted—within certain limits provided by the stiffening nudges of sticklers which every church has, and suffers from in my view.

There is a beauty in the celebration of the mysteries—no doubt at all. The candles before the icons, the singing, the preservation of liturgical movement—the processions, all of which have their inner meanings spiralling towards the central offering at the altar—of Christ, of the Holy Trinity. The beauty is attractive. It has a drawing power— the power of God's love and its drawing power.

Dostoevsky said, 'It is beauty that will save the world.'[7]

The shadow side is that the beauty can attract just on the aesthetic level and that becomes thin unless the beauty draws us to the strong mercy of God's love and to how our participation in divine things leads to our deification. 'Deification' is a strong and demanding word in Orthodoxy that resonates with the western word, Sanctification.

## Let go. Let be. Let God.

The deep beauty and meaning of Orthodox worship has been good for me. Western forms to which I shall always owe so much had become thin with their restless search for 'relevance' and were beginning to float over the top of my experience, as I said in my introduction. This Liturgy got right underneath all that I was working with as a psychotherapist— people's pathologies of soul, of psyche, addictive compulsive habits, existential anxieties, and my own symptoms and nightmares and failures

---

[7] A statement attributed to Prince Myshkin by Ippolit in Fyodor Dostoevsky, *The Idiot*, trans. Constance Garnett (New York: Bantam, 1981), 370.

in love. I could let them all go into the Liturgy and find myself sustained from a very deep level. It was nourishing and challenging. I sometimes say that it made an honest woman out of me—not to live in the two language and experience worlds of depth psychology and faith, but being called, led, driven to bring them together. But that is another story. Sometimes the mixture can seem very rich, like too much Christmas pudding. But as one learns to let go and let be and let God… one finds the deep internal rhythms of the liturgical life almost as deepening as inner silence. One begins to understand that it all sustains me rather than me having to sustain it. It understands me and I do not always have to understand it. And anyway what is called this *cataphatic* way, the way of affirmation and use of images, is all the time opened into the *apophatic* way—the way of living from the mysteries of divine Love, Truth, and Mercy, that are beyond all concepts and words. I feel the Servants of Christ the King understands that interaction of the two ways in your practice.

I wish we had time to meditate together on how you experience those same opposites in your church… in your life. Orthodox worship is full of rich ritual, and yet its theology and its prayer-teaching is mystical. It has not got the history of defining things in legalistic terms which have so often beset the western tradition. There is an amazing emphasis on Freedom, while knowing from social and historical experience of suffering and martyrdom, as well as from the life of Christ, that the deepest freedom can come from our choosing that which is ineluctably laid upon us.

It is traditional yet free, because each generation must know this renewing power of the Spirit to state the truth in its generation—yet *not* reduce it in an attempt at so-called 'relevance'.

It is archaic, unreformed in its forms, yet so alive in its practice. But of course customary practice can turn ritual and how things are supposed to be done into what Paul Evdokimov calls a 'suit of armour' guarding us from the living spirit, and Fr Lev called 'a layer of dust'. So the daily invocation of the Spirit in this prayer used daily is so important.

Each day we say:

O heavenly King, O Comforter, The Spirit of Truth, which art in all places, and fillest all things, Treasury of blessings and Giver of Life, Come and abide in us. Cleanse us from all impurity and of thy goodness save our souls.

Each day the Spirit says in us:

I call heaven and earth to witness against you today that I have set before you life and death, blessings and curses. Choose life so that you and your descendants may live, loving the Lord your God, obeying him, and holding fast to him. (Deut. 30:19–20)

There is a great emphasis on the Holy Spirit and on lived personal experience and direct invocation of the Spirit in Orthodoxy. There is the *epiclesis*—invocation—in the Liturgy, the calling down of the Spirit to change bread and wine into the Body and Blood of Christ.

The Liturgy, the sacramental life, is central to Orthodox spirituality. It is said that we fall alone, but cannot rise alone. We need the life in the Body of Christ which is our shared spiritual food, helping us to participate in new life in Christ. *Sobornost* is the Slavonic word used to describe the essential catholicity of the communal life. It can be used as an idealization—but it is also how it *is* what we do.[8]

A celebration of what is meant by *sobornost* can be found at the beginning of St Maximos the Confessor's *Mystagogia*: a work that contains, but is more than, a commentary on the Divine Liturgy:[9]

---

[8] [From this point on in the typescript there are several passages that simply repeat, word for word, what Wendy has already said. It is not likely that Wendy repeated herself to that extent, so I have traced a thread from the remarkable passage from St Maximos quoted by Wendy, which could be regarded as expounding the meaning of *sobornost*, quoting it in a slightly fuller version than in the SCK pamphlet, to bring out more clearly its cosmic and metaphysical dimensions, which were so important to Wendy—and leading the text back to her further reflections on what she had learned from Fr Lev Gillet. Ed.]

[9] [St Maximos the Confessor (*c.* 580–662) is perhaps the greatest of all Byzantine theologians. He became a monk and later in his life was embroiled in the Monothelete controversy: the doctrine that, though Christ had two natures, divine and human, he had only one (Divine) will, an 'ecumenical'

It is in this way that the holy Church of God will be shown to be active among us in the same way as God, as an image reflects its archetype. For many and of nearly boundless number are the men, women and children who are distinct from one another and vastly different by birth and appearance, by race and language, by way of life and age, by opinions and skills, by manners and customs, by pursuits and studies, and still again by reputation, fortune, characteristics and habits: all are born into the Church and through it are reborn and recreated in the Spirit. To all in equal measures the Church gives and bestows one divine form and designation: to be Christ's and to bear his name. In accordance with faith it gives to all a single, simple, whole and indivisible condition which does not allow us to bring to mind the existence of the myriads of differences among them, even if they do exist, through the universal relationship and union of all things with it. It is through the Church that absolutely no one at all is in himself separated from the community since everyone converges with all the rest and joins together with them by the one, simple, and indivisible grace and power of faith. 'For all,' it is said, 'had but one heart and one mind.' Thus … Christ himself, our true head, who … 'is all and in all' … encloses in himself all beings by the unique, simple and infinitely wise power of his goodness. As a centre of straight lines that radiate from him by his unique, simple, and single cause and power he prevents beings with the same beginning from diverging at the periphery, but rather he circumscribes their extension in a circle and brings back to himself the distinct beings brought into existence by him, so that the creations of the one God

---

compromise with those called Monophysites who rejected the Council of Chalcedon (AD 451). Since this doctrine was proclaimed in an imperial decree, Maximos' unbending opposition to it—and his drawing into the controversy the support of Pope Martin of Rome—was deemed seditious, and led to his arrest and exile to Lazica (in modern Georgia), where he soon died of his ill treatment on 13 August 662. Immediately venerated locally as a confessor, his doctrine, though not his person, was vindicated at the Sixth Ecumenical Council held in Constantinople in 681. His earlier writings concern prayer and mysticism, combining a cosmic vision with personal asceticism. Ed.]

may not live as strangers or as enemies one with another by dint of
having no reason or place in common, where they may display
their love and their peace, nor run the risk of being separated from
God and thus dissolving into nonbeing.[10]

This long quotation brings out the cosmic and metaphysical dimensions of *sobornost*, that seem to me so important. The balance and
coherence of the cosmos as God's creation are expressive of the beauty
that God's love has bestowed on the created order: a beauty that is attractive—'it is beauty that will save the world' (Dostoevsky)—that draws all
to itself, 'with the drawing of this Love and the voice of this Calling'.

Let us turn again to Fr Lev Gillet—dear Fr Lev, that passionate
deep priest and monk, most Gallic in his speech rhythms and in his wit,
who taught so many of us how to begin practising the Jesus Prayer.
How much I owe to him!

Let us see what he says:

We Orthodox are very good at worship but our interactional and eth-
nically-based politics often stink. The internal rows which are not
about the shared faith and worship but about church power-politics
and jurisdictional quarrels are very dark and often very bitter, where
no-one has any right to see themselves as doing it well. Here we are
all desperate sinners. If only this desperation would turn us to God
rather than just turn on each other!

Those profound antinomies that Fr Lev sets out are so true and do
define something about our traditional but also archaic Orthodox spirituality: traditional, archaic, personal, and mystical.

The central dogmas—belief in the Holy Trinity and in the
Incarnation of the God Man—underpin the spirituality of the Church.
The 'tradition' on these things goes continually back to the Fathers,
saints, martyrs, and early councils of the Church. In fact, one of the differences for me is the sense of living in a much more inhabited Church,

---

[10] *Mystagogia* 1, ll. 163–98, ed. Christian Boudignon in Corpus Christianorum
Series Graeca 69 (Turnhout: Brepols, 2011), somewhat condensed.
[Translation mine. Ed.]

where the apostles and saints are still with us. The 'communion of saints' is a living reality. I glimpsed this before in Catholic Anglicanism, but it has become more of a simple fact. Perhaps that centres, too, on the presence of the Mother of God, Mary. Orthodoxy has no dogmas about Mary. She is experienced as what is called 'the flower and fruit of worship ripened in tradition'. Her prayer for and with us, her presence acknowledged at the end of every litany just before we turn to Christ—these are part of life in the Church.[11]

Fr Lev's phrase—*knows as no other how to sing the joys of Pascha*— is most true in my experience. There is traditional fasting in Lent. There is a wonderful living through the Passion in Holy Week, with all its anomalies, through the Cross. And yet there is a most extraordinary climax for the Resurrection. Something happens. Christ is RISEN and celebrated, and all are called to the wedding feast. Resurrection is a central belief and experience in Orthodoxy.

There is an Orthodox saying that if we don't want change we plead 'Tradition'. If we do want change we plead *oikonomia* ('economy': pastoral discernment of the current situation).

There is also a cosmic emphasis which is expressed liturgically in many ways but particularly in the celebration of Transfiguration— showing us the state to which we are called 'from glory to glory' in the transfigured Christ—matter in its true glory. We are all called to the transfigured life.

There is also the wonderful Theophany service in January, which, at the Great Blessing of the Waters, all creation is called in—Sun, Moon, Stars, Heights and Depths, all the Cosmos and the 'Dragons of the Deep'. And then the life-giving Cross is plunged into the waters, three times, to represent new life not just for us but for the whole cosmos in Christ. There is much food for thought here for the tragedies facing us

---

[11] I tried to write about this in my contribution to the *Festschrift* for Bishop Kallistos: 'Mary, the Flower and Fruit of Worship: The Mother of God in the Orthodox Tradition', in *Abba: The Tradition of Orthodoxy in the West. Festschrift for Bishop Kallistos Ware*, ed. John Behr, Andrew Louth, Dimitri Conomos (Crestwood, NY: SVSP, 2003), 193–205. [Included below on pp. 93–108. Ed.]

through global warming and our eco-destructiveness. It is an experience of the *nexus mysteriorum*—the way all truths interact and cohere.

There is no avoidance of the dark—of sin and of the abyss of the human creature made in the image of God and needing to throw him or herself into the abyss of God's mercy. There is an emphasis on asceticism which may be daunting and can go wrong if presented as a moralism.

There is a particular emphasis, as we have mentioned, in the Russian Orthodox tradition on what they call in Slavonic *umilenie*—tender loving compassion in all humility, an acknowledgment of what makes us truly lovingly human together.

The most common practice in personal prayer is that of the Jesus Prayer—the Spirit helps us to cry:

*Lord Jesus Christ, Son of the living God, have mercy on me, a sinner.*[12]

The Jesus Prayer is not a mantra. It is an invocation; a prayer to the Lord Jesus Christ, which the Spirit can pray in us. At first I was not sure of it and certainly for many it is interspersed with other forms of personal prayer.

Each Easter midnight Resurrection happens, and the following brief homily, attributed to St John Chrysostom, is always read:

> If any be a devout lover of God, let him partake with gladness from this fair and radiant feast.
> If any be a faithful servant, let him enter rejoicing into the joy of his Lord.
> If any have wearied himself with fasting let him now enjoy his reward.
>
> If any have laboured from the first hour, let him receive today his rightful reward. If any have come after the third hour, let him celebrate the feast with thankfulness. If any have arrived after the sixth hour, let him not be in doubt, for he will suffer no loss. If any have delayed until the ninth hour, let him not hesitate but draw near. If any have arrived only at the eleventh hour, let him not be afraid because he comes so late. For the Master is generous and accepts the last even as the first. He gives rest to him who comes at the eleventh hour in the same way

---

[12] Or: 'Lord Jesus Christ, Son of God, have mercy on me, a sinner'. [See above, n. 2. Ed.]

as to him who has laboured from the first. He accepts the deed, and commends the intention.

Enter then, all of you, into the joy of the Lord. First and Last, receive alike your reward. Rich and Poor, dance together. You who have fasted and you who have not fasted, rejoice today. The table is laden, let all enjoy it. The calf is fatted; let none go hungry.

Let none lament his poverty; for the universal Kingdom is revealed. Let none bewail is transgressions; for the light of forgiveness has risen from the tomb. Let none fear death; for the death of the Saviour has set us free.

> He has destroyed death by undergoing death.
> He has despoiled hell by descending into hell.
> Hell was filled with bitterness, when it met thee face to face below;
>> filled with bitterness, for it was brought to nothing;
>> filled with bitterness, for it was mocked;
>> filled with bitterness, for it was overthrown;
>> filled with bitterness, for it was put in chains.
> It received a body, and encountered God.
> It received earth, and confronted heaven.
> O Death, where is thy sting? O Hell, where is thy victory?
>> Christ is risen, and thou art cast down;
>> Christ is risen, and the demons are fallen;
>> Christ is risen, and the angels rejoice;
>> Christ is risen, and life reigns in freedom;
>> Christ is risen, and there is none left dead in the tomb.

For Christ, being raised from the dead, has become the first-fruits of them that slept. To him be glory and dominion to the ages of ages.

Amen.

We have come, in the West, to decry the emphasis in some kinds of theology on being humble, wretched sinners, more concerned with suffering and self-imposed crosses. But as I get older, I am more sure about starting there. Where else? A sinner. 'Here I am, Lord. What a mess!' In this strange, wonderful, and terrifying universe, in which the human family lives, I need to immerse myself in Romans 8 and the

Spirit who prays in us with 'groanings that cannot be uttered'. And call out to God as the Jesus Prayer does. Fr Lev's little green book, recommended by Gonville, helped me most.[13]

I am so grateful for my past—in an evangelical conversion, for the years with the Quakers, and then through Gonville to a catholic Anglican path in a movement towards what became Orthodoxy. All this might make me into a walking ecumenical movement! But to all, including what I have learnt and now practise from the Servants of Christ the King, to ALL I am beholden and truly grateful.

But gradually, because it was following me, I could relax into it and found Orthodoxy my place—a place of Encounter, opening the deep centre of the heart, so prominent in our icons; the place of encounter with the living Christ.

---

[13] A Monk of the Eastern Church [Fr Lev's pen-name], *On the Invocation of the Name of Jesus*. [The hardback of the original English version, published by the Fellowship of St Alban and St Sergius, was bound in green cloth. Wendy is also alluding, playfully, to the 'small pea-green clothbound book' that Franny had in her handbag in J. D. Salinger's novel *Franny and Zooey*: that pea-green book was R. M. French's translation of the anonymous Russian work, *The Way of a Pilgrim*, which is also about the Jesus Prayer. Its mention in Salinger's novel lent it a certain fame in the 1960s. Wendy did better with Fr Lev's book (now available in an expanded form as *The Jesus Prayer*). Ed.]

# THE QUEST FOR THE HEART OF THE WORK: AN ONTOLOGICAL APPROACH TO SPIRITUALITY AND PSYCHOTHERAPY/COUNSELLING

## NOTE

This paper was first given as a talk to the graduate body of the Westminster Pastoral Foundation in London. In its origins, over twenty years ago, the Foundation wanted to remain true to its roots in the Judaeo-Christian tradition and to develop good pastoral counselling with professional development in psychodynamic theory and practice.

## *Prolegomena on Form*

In this article I use a visual metaphor to express, in its gradually constructed form, something of the subject matter I will present. I use a stone with a hole through it as the central focus. Around it I gradually place other circling stones. I want to present certain ideas, but to leave plenty of space between them for the ideas of others. I want to convey the feeling of an open field of discourse, with much space and silence and room to move for others, who might come from very different psychological and spiritual backgrounds from my own—and yet at the same time I want to locate firmly, through the stones, certain of my deepest concerns.

Colleagues and students, particularly women, in psychotherapy, counselling, theology and spirituality often speak of how daunted they are by the customary forms and language in which our professional and theoretical writings are presented. They do not seem to present the 'truth to the material' of which sculptors speak; they do not encourage varied forms of creative writing. Psychoanalysis, in all its schools, has had a profound effect on artistic form, to allow for the generative effect of unconscious energies in the creative process. Why are we, who work with unconscious material all the time, so tied to modernistic rationalism and prescribed forms? This is a *cri de coeur*, for I mourn for the loss of so much of the wisdom of the 'oral tradition' in which we all work, a tradition that cannot find written form.

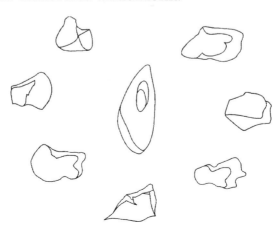

# FINDING A WAY IN

Years ago, when we lived in Central Africa, we heard a story about a white man who was on a journey with African carriers. He knew he had made a fair deal with them, so he was amazed when, three days into the journey, they went on strike. When they were asked why, they replied: 'We have been travelling a long time; now we must sit and wait for our souls to catch up.' I have been reminded of this story because a marked feature of the last few years is that spirituality has been allowed out of the psychotherapy closet. Are we at last allowing something to catch up? Is a new social phenomenon occurring among us? Perhaps we are ready to find new dimensions of the soul's ability to act as a mediator between spirit and matter/body.

However, the deep psyche is shy and elusive — the butterfly of the ancient Greek symbol. The spirit blows where it lists. The body is an opaque, tacit dimension of our experience and a multivalent carrier of symbolic meanings that operate between the individual body and the social body.[1] When we include 'spirituality', the 'quest for the heart of our work' becomes subtle and taxing, requiring as much silence as words. Faced with the post-modern hypermarket of 'spiritualities' (forms in which the life of the spirit might be explored), I become reticent and resistant and want to close my eyes and my mouth and plunge into the depths of the Judaeo-Christian tradition to which I belong. If we are going to embark on the vast oceans of different religions and spiritual traditions and try to sound their depths in new ways, in relation to the depths of the differing psychodynamic traditions, then we are liable to break up on the rocks of our differences.

---

[1] Mary Douglas, *Natural Symbols: Explorations in Cosmology* (The Cresset Press, London: Barrie & Rockcliffe, 1970).

In 1997 the Oxford Psychotherapy Society held a meeting addressed by a leading psychoanalyst and a bishop of the Church of England on the theme 'Facing the Void'. During the subsequent discussion it became apparent to many people that the Void was being experienced between the two 'worlds' represented by the speakers and among us as colleagues because of our different beliefs and presuppositions. Some of us realized then that deep and stormy waters lay ahead of any attempt to embark on a prolonged exploration of spirituality and psychotherapy. As we try to see what it would mean even to push a boat out into those waters, I take heart from the courses on 'Counselling and Ontology' which David Holt, a Jungian analytical psychologist, and then he and I together and separately ran at the Westminster Pastoral Foundation (WPF). We searched long and hard for a word that could hold for us the necessary sustained attention to the mystery of being and human being. We believed that this mystery always surpasses and eludes our attempts both to know all about things, and the theories and methodologies in psychodynamic work that guide us as to how to do something with what is presented to us. Eventually we settled, with a sense of gravity and perhaps foolhardiness, on a word with a long philosophical history — ontology: the science and study of being. We knew that we would have to work with a plurality of beliefs and their possible conflicts. We hoped our psychodynamic trainings would help. The difficulties proved enormous but the task worthwhile. We knew that our groups were a microcosm of problems current in the society in which we live. 'Ontology' expressed a desire to explore in disciplined ways the necessary tension between the language worlds drawn from the faith in which WPF was founded and from the psychoanalytic traditions which informed WPF's professional involvement in counselling and psychotherapy. It opened up areas of personal (individual and social) experience that transcend and subvert divisions that are made between the two worlds and often involved a cross-critique between them. It meant working in a state of creative tension between basic beliefs about the 'spirit' and the philosophical presuppositions of psychoanalytic theories, with each constantly questioning the other.

Sometimes discussion seemed pulled to the point of almost unbearable tension between the opposites. There was always the danger of collapse into warring factions, with the possibility of expulsions, exclusions or uneasy occlusions. Sometimes there was a mysterious creative emergence, a transformative touch of the Spirit which took us all into new places. I used to say to the students that ontology was making an honest woman out of me—bringing about a complex, challenging and often conflictual marriage between the worlds that I had all too often kept separate for the sake of a somewhat dishonest peace.

I want to set out some of the issues which became and have remained focal for me. To do that I shift my metaphor from deep waters to the earth to the stone metaphor alluded to in the opening section of this article. The issues held by the stones are for me waymarkers, presences to which I return with a sense of wonder and mystery, touchstones for the realities that I want to witness. They give me some sense of orientation, with much mapping still to be done, in an ontological approach forged to try to keep spirituality and psychotherapy 'sounding' together, whatever the harmonies or dissonances involved.

## CENTRAL STONE
### A Sense of Mystery

I place at the centre a stone with a hole in the middle, rather like a Barbara Hepworth sculpture. I want it to convey that at the heart of our work there will always be a sense of mystery, of the unknown-yet-present, a sense of wonder at Being. We are called to attend to that mystery.

On the painter Paul Klee's simple tombstone there are words inscribed that tell how his life and work moved him: 'Somewhat nearer than usual to the heart of creation but still too far away.' That speaks to my condition. In the quest for the heart of the work I know that in all the nearness I am still too far away. And yet, sometimes when I feel very far away, the nearness is there. Often it is art, music, poetry, sculpture, the dream, that take some of us nearer to the heart of our work by remaining true to the mystery of the transcendent unknown, as when in

Richard Wilbur's poem we are 'touched with ocean'.[2] It often strikes me with a sense of irony that we psychotherapists and counsellors have become somewhat 'knowing' about the unknown. We lay down methods and theories and doctrines about the structures of deep subjectivity and ways of working with them, and there is a constant danger that they may become defences against the unknown and the mystery at the heart of the work. Interpretations which seek to transfer all experiences which a client might express in terms of spiritual and religious experience into psychodynamically understood patterns of the developmental life cycle of the individual—as if the former were mere epiphenomena and an avoidance of the 'nitty-gritty' and the latter more 'real' (phrases I have heard often enough)—need challenging, if spirituality and psychotherapy are to be in meaningful dialogue. Spiritual traditions as well as psychodynamic theories have ways of dealing with illusion, denial and avoidance. Dialogue, including fundamental disagreement and conflict, can be very fruitful—and sometimes frighteningly sterile or abortive. We found in discussions on ontology and counselling that there are often very wide discrepancies between what people were prepared to countenance as 'real', 'more real', 'unreal' in human experience. I might point out that this is also part of the history of theology in relation to religious experience. There is always the spiritual tension between not wanting to be obscurantist about what can be known and yet not wanting to be iconoclastic about what is sacred.

*STONE ONE*
## The Danger of Ontological Collapse

How can we honour the mystery at the heart of the work? I believe it is by forms of attention that we can 'let be'. Such are akin to prayer, contemplation, meditation and wise silence: they do not always seek to interpret in a 'knowing' way. I know that in our professional work we

---

[2] Richard Wilbur, *Collected Poems 1943–2004*, Harvest Books (New York: Harcourt, Brace & Co., 1989), 211.

are taught to respect the client's way of talking about their experience. There are, however, selective processes involved in what we focus on, how we attend to it—and how we reframe it. Some clients and some counsellors in supervision comment on ways in which their spiritual and religious ways of formulating their experience are consistently re-framed, so that they learn to bracket them out. A colleague of mine did a research project around a question to colleagues: 'Do you pray for your clients?'[3] She found a significant degree of anxiety about what it would mean to admit the practice of prayer, in terms of how it might be understood within the profession, by clients, colleagues—and par-ticularly by supervisors. There are forms of attention that can honour the sense of Presence (of the Divine) on which life itself and the soul depend for their very existence. Here I would want to stand with George Steiner against a post-modernist stance.[4] We particularly need forms of attention that refuse to over-interpret, or to displace a fullness of meaning onto an alternative story, denying the presence of the tran-scendent Other. Encouraging imaginative creative expression rather than over-interpretation involves a dwelling in and on symbols and their transformations.

If we fail to attend to the mystery at the heart of things, then we stand in great danger of ontological collapse. If there is a spiritual/di-vine dimension to being, transcendent to and immanent in all being—if we are created for awareness of our CAPAX DEI, our capacity for God—then we need to recognize and allow for that dimension in our work. Unrecognized, there is an all-too-apparent danger that the energies of that dimension of being will be collapsed and displaced onto other levels that cannot bear the weight. I believe that, when that is happen-ing, social structures, the family, marriage, relationships, children and individual lives are burdened with weights of meaning that they cannot

---

[3] Jessica Rose, *A Needle-Quivering Poise: Between Prayer and Practice in the Counselling Relationship*, Contact Pastoral Monograph 6 (Contact Pastoral Trust Limited, 1996).

[4] George Steiner, *Real Presences* (London: Faber & Faber, 1989).

carry without danger of collapse. Concern about this collapse in our society and our psychoanalytic culture gives a sense of urgency to our need to examine our philosophical presuppositions, and to understand that what happens in transference and countertransference is altogether more serious than our current theories allow. I have to confess that, when I read my way into the reductions involved in our theorizing about the human condition, I begin to suffer from claustrophobia and start gasping for air — for the breath of the Spirit.

*STONE TWO*
## The History of Desire

Spiritual traditions and the psychoanalytic traditions both have much to say about the history of desire as we seek or are driven to participate in and sound the depths of love. I owe to the psychoanalytic tradition a rich awareness of desire for the other. I have learnt much from it about Eros — sexuality in all its myriad forms and vicissitudes — familial, creative, destructive, embodied, diverted, engendered.

Ontology reminds me that desire has a teleological, a purposive pull towards its own transcendence, as it responds to a call that is beyond all the forms of immediacy. If lack, or want, is the beginning of desire, then lack is endless because desire is in the end desire for God, the Divine, the Eternal Thou — the source and end of love and the very energy of love itself at work in creation, in the teeth of all the evidence to the contrary.

How can I remain true to St Augustine's famous phrase, 'Our hearts are restless until they find their rest in you',[5] while at the same time 'staying with' all the kinds of work that I do professionally about the workings of desire? At least I can allow deeper questions on the nature of desire and our journey into love and not collapse too much meaning into human relationships themselves. Realizing that desire is endless and divine in its intent means that at least we do not seek an

---

[5] *Confessions*, 1:1.

impossible fulfilment from each other. We can learn to let be, while seeking ways of becoming. Working with clients within a wide spiritual as well as psychodynamic frame of reference has opened up for me new ways of focusing questioning around desire, its energies and possible transformations, so that meanings connected with social and spiritual aspects of the 'history of desire' can be addressed and encouraged.

I take heart from some of the current work in spirituality as well as therapy which has the courage to tangle with gender problems. The history of desire takes on new dimensions as women begin to discover feminine forms of spirit and soul. Women mystics have often expressed their experiences of the divine in daring and often dizzyingly erotic language. Attention to them can bring a refreshing glimpse of lands of far distances to be explored which can change our more confined struggles with the addictions and compulsions involved in the demands that we can inadvisedly place upon an all-too-human other. Ontological collapse in the realm of 'the history of desire' has a devastating effect.

*STONE THREE*
## The Mystery of Origins and Ends

Ontology in relation to my work has often immersed me in the essential mystery of our origins and our ends, neither of which are in our hand, and has opened me up to 'the beyond in the midst'. It is here that great religious traditions with their developed practices, narratives and beliefs have reached out into areas beyond our 'knowing'. Psychotherapy has an obsession with origins and theories based on the aetiological causality of adult ills in early childhood. We use, often effectively, more and more complex constructs about the nature of early experience. We sometimes seem totally preoccupied with a kind of archaeological horizon, so that we stand in danger of occluding the many areas of human experience that need a teleological, purposive horizon to give them their due value in making for mature adulthood.

There are times in my work when I feel attuned to Ernest Becker's *The Denial of Death*.[6] How far are some of our theoretical preoccupations, if we examine their presuppositions, a participation in the Zeitgeist and a consistent denial of death? Death, as Becker says, makes us question, in ways we would prefer to deny, our *causa sui* project, our assumption that we are in control and do not need God.

A sense of finitude, our mortality, opens up unknown levels of being. Our work changes so much when we are trying to stay with a client who is dying. This is quite different from working with those clients who feel that life is a terminal illness. I remember one client who came from a family with a terrible history of suicide. We worked for a long time with her conviction that one day she would be driven to accept the family fate and commit suicide herself. Then one day she found she had an inoperable cancer. I remember how she said to me, 'I have discovered that I do not want to die. Only now do I want to accept the gift of life. Help me to live as I die.'

I have noticed over the years how often clients who have had a tremendous struggle to come to terms with 'the accident of their birth' and consequent traumatic experiences will sometimes bring me a new level of being in themselves when they come across, or re-read, 'with a circumcised eye', verses like those of Psalm 139:13–16: 'when you created my inmost being, you knit me together in my mother's womb … My frame was not hidden from you when I was made in the secret place. When I was woven together in the depths of the earth, your eyes saw my unformed body.' They discover that there is more to origin than a thoughtless act, an attempted abortion or not being wanted.

Sometimes, when I have been in a vulnerable place over my own children, or over a death, or the sudden death of a colleague and all its aftermath, or the onset of a grave illness, or an accident, I have been alarmed at the casually interpretative remarks of some colleagues, as if there existed a 'knowing' to which we had access, as if there were always

---

[6] Ernest Becker, *The Denial of Death* (New York: The Free Press; London: Macmillan, 1973).

some simple causal continuity instead of ruptures and tragedies and the inexplicable. I remember my gratitude for a comment of David Holt's on 'the ontological status of accident'. Life is too mysterious, and often much too painful, as it carries its shadow of finitude to be treated thus. The why and the how of things does not always equal the what. That things are just the way they are is the more mysterious—and demanding.

## STONE FOUR
*Paradigm Shifts*

Working from the viewpoint of ontology, which brings the spiritual and the psychotherapeutic into dialogue, I see the central need for a view of the human person that includes a social and an individual pole. It commits me to exploring the corporate and the making of community in ways that are as inclusive as possible and that are based on the lived and suffered owning of difference. The 'stone' metaphor that I am using 'holds' that for me. I also have to acknowledge that the Judaeo-Christian tradition to which I belong believes that the kingdom of God and the kingdom of this world are not the same thing, though they are inextricably in relation until the kingdom comes. But, if our professional variant of the latter becomes more and more totalizing in its view of the human condition, in ways that effectively preclude the former, then I must, from within the profession, begin to argue for much more examination of our presuppositions. Somehow I have to try to live creatively—and often painfully—with the conflict of interpretations of the human condition.

Some of the imperatives which guided the beginning of the psychotherapy profession were based on a critique of authoritarian social structures. The shadow side of that critique, as it developed in our practice, has been the too little examined promotion of individualism. Now we seem to many, not to be in critical tension with the prevailing Zeitgeist of individualism, self-fulfilment and market forces, but actually to be promoting it. There are signs that we are waking up to the social and political implications of our work, and I am grateful to those like Andrew Samuels who are intelligently discerning and who are goading us into more awareness.[7]

Thomas Kuhn reminded us of the power of paradigms—how they work and how they shift under the creative stress of new ideas.[8] He defines a paradigm as the entire constellation of ideas, beliefs, values and techniques shared by a given community, so that there comes to be a strong network of commitments, conceptual, theoretical, instrumental and methodological. Empires are built out of paradigms, vested interests are guarded. It takes courage for the creative and the prophetic to witness the anomalies in the system and find a breakthrough for the new. Every profession goes through a 'normatizing stage', with an emphasis on stabilizing knowledge and practice, emphasizing boundaries and the need to be seen to toe a line. Perhaps the psychotherapy profession is in the normatizing stage?

I shudder at the amount of time and energy we are currently using on 'professionalization' with its emphasis on powerful hierarchies, its obsession with boundaries—and exclusions. Are we not tightening up and battening down a paradigm which is shifting and needs to shift? Some of the pressures come from a changing society. Some come from what has been an all-too-tacit unease about the philosophical presuppositions from within the profession's own members, in particular, for some, their presupposition about ultimate spiritual values and realities. Of course, we need 'training'. But in our preoccupation with matters like training and qualification we seem to get into an endless pre-empting of deep issues. Many of my colleagues admit wryly that they would never have been accepted by training systems that they now have to enforce. Many colleagues learnt through apprenticeship. I remember hearing a story about Carl Rogers. He said that he had spent three decades on training issues and endless committees and had then woken up and realized that there were still as many 'quacks' and as much misconduct within

---

[7] See particularly A. Samuels, *The Political Psyche* (London: Routledge, 1993).

[8] Thomas S. Kuhn, *The Structure of Scientific Revolutions* (Chicago: University of Chicago Press, 1970).

the trained profession as without. That is a hard and no doubt arguable saying, but perhaps we need to hear it. There is necessary work to be done, but there is a danger that we of all people (given our radical origins) are running into a counter-move from outside the profession, about 'people not psychotherapy and counselling', which is perhaps the equivalent in this decade of the 'people not psychiatry' movement of the 1970s. Some of our theories and practices are being much questioned by all the recent publicity about the so-called 'recovered memory syndrome'. Perhaps the issues raised will make us get involved in the painful task of examining our presuppositions? We may complain about current media misrepresentation of our profession, but what are we in fact doing to ourselves? Can we not take a more radical look at ourselves, own some of the immense differences among us, and realize that, even as we lay our working lives on the paradigmatic line of professional orthodoxy, the spirit will be moving on and the creative people, if they have not hobbled themselves with the shackles of orthodoxy to the point of exhaustion, will have to move on too?

I remember how much my own practice was changed by a talk given by Edward Thornton, an American pastoral theologian and counsellor, at Westminster Pastoral Foundation in the 1970s. He said that his own agency in the States had been changed radically after they had introduced into their intake and assessment procedures ways of asking people openly and simply not only about their psychosexual development but also about their spiritual/philosophical development. No doubt Andrew Samuels would also include political development. What we pay attention to has an effect on our practice and theorizing. It is encouraging to think that discussion on such topics among us as colleagues, difficult and potentially divisive though they may prove, could lead to paradigmatic shifts that could renew our creativity in the profession and promote our diversity as a good to be fostered. It could also freshen up our language, bringing out of so-called psychobabble new forms of expression, in which more of our contemporaries from different disciplines and life experience could join with us in our explorations of the human condition.

## *Hermeneutics*

In work on ontology and counselling another word often begins to appear alongside ontology. This is the word 'hermeneutics': the art and science of interpretation. Our very being, the world in which we find ourselves—these are not transparent but opaque, full of the unknown and the hidden which we have to seek to find. The very nature of human reflective consciousness means that we have to indwell 'being' and 'the world' to try to interpret their meanings, even while we participate in them. Our profession is committed to an attempt to understand and interpret something of what is going on. When I use the word 'understand' I try to remember a cautionary tale from family life. One day, on a wet Welsh family holiday with our three sons, we all took shelter in a pub at lunch-time. A family fracas broke out, in the way they do. Eventually one of our sons said in raised tones: 'The trouble with this family is that my father thinks he knows everything and my mother thinks she understands everything. My trouble is, my mother "understands" me; she is a psychotherapist, you see.' I took the point and have pondered on it ever since, though when I talked to him about it recently he could not remember the incident. Such is life! But of course the business is endless. I had to understand that my son did not wish to be understood. As Winnicott said in a lecture at the London School of Economics in 1960, 'How wonderful it is to be hidden. How terrible not to be found.'

Always we must begin to understand that there is more to be understood. The interpretation of experience takes us into the hermeneutic circle. As St Anselm expressed it: 'I believe in order that I may understand.' What we believe gives us a bearing, a compass bearing on our understanding. Yet we know how differently we believe—and how much the differences can scramble our understanding of each other. How can we learn to find our bearings and yet know what it means to say, 'I surrender my point of view, I embrace the whole'?

Flannery O'Connor, that sharp, witty, incisive American author of scarifying novels about the 'Jesus-haunted South', said that she was often asked what it meant to be a Catholic novelist. She replied that she did not write about her faith but that she hoped she wrote out of it. I want that to be true of how I live my faith in my work. With people from different spiritual backgrounds I do not necessarily talk about what I believe, but I hope I work out of it. I would want, in some way, often tacit, to bear witness to it by at least not betraying it. I often fail. Pressures from within the profession and from without are subtle, and evasion is easy.

I realize that in setting out these touchstones and letting them circle in an open field I have spoken directly and indirectly about how for me the centre of the circle and the heart of the work carries within it, known or unknown and mysterious past all knowing, the presence of the living God. That means that I have to keep spirituality and psychotherapy together—sounding with and across each other. The viewpoints of any and all human beings are partial and manifold. It is only, as St Paul reminds us of a passage from the prophet Isaiah, 'the Spirit searches everything, even the depths of God' (1 Cor. 2:10; Is. 64).

# References and Further Seminal Texts

Ernest Becker, *The Denial of Death* (New York: Free Press; London: Macmillan, 1973).

Mary Douglas, *Natural Symbols: Explorations in Cosmology* (The Cresset Press, London: Barrie & Rockcliffe, 1970).

René Girard, *Violence and the Sacred* (Baltimore: Johns Hopkins University Press, 1977).

—— , *Things Hidden since the Foundation of the World* (London: Athlone Press, 1987).

David Holt, *The Psychology of Carl Jung: Essays in Application and Deconstruction* (New York and Lampeter: Edwin Mellen Press, 1992).

Thomas S. Kuhn, *The Structure of Scientific Revolutions* (Chicago: University of Chicago Press, 1970).

Paul Ricoeur, *Freud and Philosophy: An Essay in Interpretation* (New Haven CT: Yale University Press, 1970).

Jessica Rose, *A Needle-Quivering Poise: Between Prayer and Practice in the Counselling Relationship*, Contact Pastoral Monograph 6 (Edinburgh: Contact Pastoral Limited Trust, 1996).

Andrew Samuels, *The Political Psyche* (London: Routledge, 1993).

George Steiner, *Real Presences* (London: Faber & Faber, 1989).

Richard Wilbur, *Collected Poems 1943–2004*, Harvest Books (New York: Harcourt, Brace & Co., 1989).

# The Lost Traveller's Dream: Developing a Theology for Working with Mental Illness

## Out of the Rut

I have been working in the field of mental health in different capacities for about forty years now. Whenever I've come near a theologian I have badgered them to do something about providing an adequate theology for us, addressing the kind of work that we do, the kind of human suffering we meet, and the kind of situations in which we find ourselves. There hasn't been a lot of response. Then, suddenly, here I am, having been thrown into the hot seat and asked to do the theology.

You must forgive me I am not a theologian. But I have at least some kind of perspective on it, which is what I can share with you today, knowing that for every person there will be a different theology. We all have our own priorities and different ways of stating things. What matters is the interaction between us.

The trouble about theologians is that they tend to get a bit set in their ways. I like to tell a story which belongs to the time when we lived in Africa. Outside the village where we lived there was a huge road sign. It read, 'Choose your rut carefully. It will be with you for the next 90 miles.'

There is something about that. We all get into ruts, ways of looking at things, ways of thinking about things, and sometimes we have to know that lurch of coming out of the rut, and wondering if we are going to find a way forward or not.

There has been much change recently in the whole field of mental health. I have been collecting some of the comments that I have heard around the subject of change.

—Heard in an Oxford college: 'I detest all change, especially change for the better.'

—And another comment: 'Now they want change, as if things weren't bad enough already.'

—'All change is change for the worse.'

I remember the graffiti that used to be up in the Sixties, saying, 'Permanent change is here to stay.' There's some truth in that, isn't there, in the way we're living at the moment.

## *The Marriage Feast*

When I think of the image we use to describe the end of time, the marriage-feast of the Lamb, I sometimes think of the people I've known over the last forty years who are, please God, going to be at that marriage-feast. And I ask myself, 'What kind of theology, what kind of knowledge of God, is going to be there on that occasion?'

When you think about the people you are working with, the people who are going to be with us there what an extraordinary occasion it is going to be! Those enormous differences, those enormous wounds, those enormous pains. What will happen when there is that final marriage between Love and Truth? When there is enough Love and Truth to go round, so that the wounds are healed?

## *From Noise to Silence*

I have sometimes said, since I started teaching in the field of pastoral counselling, that it has been making an honest woman out of me. Those of you who have received a professional training will know how we were taught to bracket out anything to do with the language-world of faith, or God, and how deep was the divide in what we were allowed to talk about.

Somehow we need to bring these language-worlds together. As we do that, we become aware (or at least I do) that there is one thing we know for sure in trying to reflect, theologically, upon the experience of the people we work with. It is that a conviction theology, sure of itself, sure of answers, secure in its own language, is a sort of ghetto-blaster. It makes too much noise. It doesn't approximate to the vulnerability, the woundedness, the suffering, the pain, the darkness of the people we work with. It makes you wince sometimes, because it cuts through atmosphere. It has a deadening effect on things. We have to get away from it. We have to start in a small way with a quieter, more listening, more silent theology.

It is not that the people we work with have no experience of God, of the spirit, of the transcendent—whatever name they give it. Often they are immersed in it, drowned in it: 'not waving, but drowning'.[1]

The meeting and inter-penetration of the divine and human is the most intimate act of all: human intimacy is, perhaps, an image of it. If we are to understand something of that intimacy, we have to be able to move between words and silence. When we try to do so, we find it difficult, sometimes, to talk to each other.

The philosopher, Collingwood, says, 'We are all ticklish in our pre-suppositions.'[2] You know how ticklishness can be a pleasure, and make one laugh, or it can be extremely painful, and quite a sadistic thing in the end. If we tried talking in a group of any size about our theological presuppositions in the field of mental health, pretty soon we would have a 'ticklish' situation on our hands, although there would be some things we would find in common.

## Borderlands

We have to live in the borderland between experience and its interpretation: how people are to live with, work with and understand what is happening to them. We have to learn, I think, to thrive not on theoretical or theological certainties, but on the crackle and twang of ambiguities, uncertainties, on a tension pulled to the pitch of crucifixion in some peoples' lives, if we are to honour both the poetry and the prose, the prosaicness of suffering, the pain, the power of the lives lived. We have to learn that tremendous, scabrous humour which is so much part, sometimes, of the experience of people who have suffered a great deal, totally lacking in illusion.

As someone said to me recently, when talking about God, 'It is costing me my life's blood to talk to you about God. I have never, ever, said

---

[1] Stevie Smith, title and last line of her poem, 'Not Waving, but Drowning', in her *Selected Poems*, ed. James MacGibbon (Penguin, 1978), 167.
[2] R. G. Collingwood, *An Essay on Metaphysics* (London: Oxford University Press, 1940), 31.

this to anyone, not even to myself.' This was a life that had contained a good deal of suffering at the hands of God, as the person saw it.

What we are involved in, day by day, with individuals, with our groups, is privileged communication. It is a privilege to be there, to hear it. And then we have to decide what we make of it: how we talk about it together, in a way that can help us.

The philosopher Bachelard says that the image touches the depth before it stirs the surface.[3] Often we have to find a way of reflecting together, theologically, the image that can 'hold' something of what we are experiencing, long before it touches the surface where we can begin to think about it.

I want to share with you the image that has come into my mind while I have been wondering what I could say on this subject, to see if we can work from it.

## Boundary Riders

I have talked about the border-country between experience and its interpretation. The kind of theologians we have to be involves a theology of 'boundary riders', of 'wayfarers'. We need to explore what it means to live in border country, continually out on the edges of existence with other people.

When things go wrong for us as human beings, in our wounds, our anxieties, our depressions, our compulsions, our mood-seizures, our withdrawals from what it generally means to be human and in touch with others; when we meet our failures, our betrayals in love, work, creativity, play; we are driven out to the edges of existence. We feel that we are at the end of our tether, the end of our endurance. We fall into our particular—our individual—kinds of end talk. 'This is the end.' 'One more thing and something will snap inside me.' 'My world came to an end.'

---

[3] Gaston Bachelard, *The Poetics of Space* (Boston: Beacon, 1964), xii.

The inner or outer world of relative coherence, bondedness, belongingness, comes to an end, and we feel hopeless, helpless, trapped, poor in spirit, dispirited, marginal. We have to learn what it means to live in the margins ourselves, and to share the very jagged sense of margins in which so many of those we work with live.

We would like to stop the world and get *off*, and the step for many people would not be a big one. We uncover those jagged edges in us when we are broken, sick, hurt, damaged. We have to learn what it means to live there. If we survive, and find a means, a way, or the way finds us so that we can grow some scar tissue, or learn how to live with mortal wounds, we can sometimes then be alongside others, and ride the bounds with them: those lonely, dark, deep places of unknowing of the human heart.

Someone said to me once, 'God made the first world out of chaos, so I suppose I shall have to do that, too.'

So we need a theology for boundary riders, wayfarers, those who have to stay out in those places with others, where God, if God is experienced at all, is usually incognito, in disguise; where He is spoken of, if at all, with great care; and where to live the questions of the suffering which people endure, is to do theology. They are places of sudden encounter and exchange, which can be surprising, or shocking; where suddenly there is a meeting or encounter in Love and in Truth, so that one can't get outside it and wonder what is happening. It's not possible to know which is us and which is God, and what exactly is going on in theological terms, but only that there is Love, there is Truth, there is meeting: something has happened between two people.

We have to stay in there, and learn to speak of You, the eternal You, corning to meet us. Those places where God is experienced as the Beyond in the midst so deeply in the midst as to be inseparable from it.

Those who are most seriously damaged and afflicted live in the borderlands, on the boundaries, the edges of existence. Sometimes there is an odd oasis, one of those meeting-places where people can feel at home. Mostly, as we know, people when they are deeply afflicted do not feel at home in the world, but share with Housman that sense of 'I, a stranger and afraid / In a world I never made.'[4]

They have a longing for the centre of things, but always feel off-centre, slewed, skewed, peripheral.

## Clearing the Line

Between the margins of existence and what is believed to be the centre (always experienced as elsewhere), there is a baffle, a scrambler, a cow on the line, so that communication can't get through easily, or at all, because damaged relationships prevent the communication channels from remaining clear.

So much of what is experienced there is unspeakable, because it is unutterable.

When we think of the kind of experiences people have had, we know how a human condition can have that tragic dimension to it where things are unutterable. Things that should never, ever, happen to a human being have happened to so many people that we know.

That kind of unspeakable unutterableness is pent up in people, forcing its way towards utterance in a vulnerable birth, a breakdown of tears Heaven knows what manifestation. Or it can feel like Yeats's monster 'slouching towards Bethlehem', waiting to be born and bringing great fear with it.[5]

The edges of existence are also the edges of language, where words fail, or become vehement, aggressive verbal acts; where silence too can be fraught, weighted with danger, shrouded in ungovernable moods and occasional bouts of incomprehensible or violent action.

There is a special relationship between the boundary, the edges of existence, and the centre: an apprehension of how it must or should be, an unconscious experience, perhaps, of the God whose centre is everywhere and circumference nowhere.

---

[4] A. E. Housman, *Collected Poems* (London: Cape, 1959), 111.
[5] W. B. Yeats, *Collected Poems* (Dublin: Macmillan, 1982), 211.

## Prophets among the Afflicted

Among the afflicted arise the prophets whose voice cannot be heard. Some of the people we know are prophetic about what is happening in this world. Some are major, some minor, some reluctant prophets like Jonah in the belly of the whale, shut up with all those digestive juices, trying to make some sense of things. And some, of course, are self-appointed prophets, who are never easy to live with in any group situation.

The trouble is that the powerful, critical acumen of the afflicted is often experienced as negative and destructive, so that we shut our ears and eventually refuse to hear it. It tends to be absolutist. It is all or nothing. 'If you cannot give me who has nothing the all, you are giving me nothing.'

It is searingly, offensively, brutally honest. And it can release the offensive stink in our cant and hypocrisy, in society as well as in the church. It can reveal how brittle and shallow is the patching-up with sticking plaster that our treatment methods and our theoretical frameworks attempt, when the wounds are so gaping.

Between the edges of existence and the centre, there is a special trajectory of desire, or longing. But of course in worldly terms, the most afflicted, the most critically prophetic, are not appointed to the places of influence and authority. They remain for us uncomfortable, sometimes uncouth pilgrims of the absolute, victims of a sort of nihilism that can lie at the heart of our societies. What we have to do is to witness, witness, witness what they share with us about how things are, before God and others, and not pretend it is otherwise.

## Survival Skills

To be boundary riders, to choose to live with affliction in the borderlands, requires, it seems to me, highly differentiated survival skills. Borderlands, boundaries, edges are places of terror and devastation, and also places of rare, even unique, shy, heart-rending beauty. Think of your encounters with some of the people you know who have suffered most, and those moments that are so beautiful. The opposites can be experienced there in their utmost tension and most vibrant co-inherence, when things suddenly come together.

Paul Ricoeur, the theologian-philosopher, calls them the places of 'rupture and suture', where things break open and where things are sewn together, between ourselves, he says, 'and what appears as the wholly Other'.[6]

The Quaker, William Penn, uses another metaphor: 'Where is the poison, there is the antidote.'[7] Unless we can learn to stay with where the suffering is, where the darkness is, where the wounds are, we cannot find the antidote.

It is where and when we come apart that God the transcendent can reach us, where occasionally we hear, as Berger said, 'the rumour of angels'.[8] Or, as someone else said, 'We are watching for the sentinels of the horizon.' Just occasionally, if we watch and listen carefully enough, we hear that rumour of angels.

What helps to steady the nerve in this lonely place? What helps us to remain men and women of spirit in these dark and difficult places to which people sometimes take us?

Someone came to me the other day and said, 'I've come to you because people have said that you are willing to talk about God. I believe in God. But the trouble is He smashes me. Either I end up thinking I am God, or, at the other extreme, that there is no room for me at all in God's world. So what can you tell me about that?'

The rest of us learn to cover up our inclinations to believe that we are God. I can tell you a story about a bishop at a conference, who stood up to give the final sermon, and said how much he had learned from the conference, how much he had enjoyed being there, and said that he

---

[6] Paul Ricoeur, *Freud and Philosophy* (New Haven: Yale University Press, 1970), 526.

[7] William Penn, *Christian Faith and Practice in the Experience of the Society of Friends*, Yearly Meeting of the Religious Society of Friends (London: Religious Society of Friends, 1960), section 183.

[8] Peter Berger, *Rumour of Angels* (London: Pelican, 1971).

felt he had everything to learn about how to be still and 'know that I am God'! The truth will out…

Another person I saw recently, the child of missionary parents, said, 'Oh, yes, I believe in God. I can't do anything other. All I know is that He will always say no to everything that I want, whether it is love, whether it is presents, or whatever it is.'

## Right Answers, Wrong Questions

Such people remind me of that saying, 'You Christians know the answers, but they are not the answers to my questions.'

What are the questions that people are asking us, theologically? How do we find spirit in the valley of dry bones, in the wasteland of broken images? No mean task. Our work there forms, and re-forms, and de-forms us. How deformed do any of us feel we are by the kind of work we have to do? There are all kinds of ways, I think.

All our professional jargon, our ways of trying to hold our act together, cannot altogether domesticate the wild thing that we have stalked, sometimes to our peril.

If we are to remain people of spirit, we have to be aware of the way the Holy Spirit seems to have at least two speeds and everything in between: that sometimes there can be a lightning-flash of healing and restoration, but more often it seems like Dead Slow, or Stop; that something goes on for a very, very long time sometimes for a whole lifetime, because the wounds are so deep.

## Spirit and Place

David Jones, the poet, talks about a spirit as a 'genius loci',[9] the spirit of each place, whom we need, for the spirit is 'a rare one for locality'. The spirit meets in a place, a person. And each place is different, he says, 'where all the stones of demarcation dance and interchange, and need recognition'. How can we recognize together what is happening?

---

[9] David Jones, *The Sleeping Lord & other Poems* (London: Faber & Faber, 1974), 59.

I believe that we need ways of talking and praying and worshipping in groups where we can witness to what we have found in our work, and recognize because the witness is an orienteer who has learned as much that the map is not the territory. The theories are there, the theologies are there, but this is the territory, and it doesn't quite fit. We've got to share and try to witness together about what we have found, in order to orientate ourselves.

I am haunted by David Jones' image in that poem when he says we have to learn 'to laugh in the mantle of variety'.[10] There is never an overall answer. There is only the variety of answers, the personal particularity of answers and encounters. So the spirit takes us to laugh in the mantle of variety.

## Finding Christ

How do we find Christ in those places? I think we have to turn to the body. What painful exchanges are experienced by the body, if am someone who is deeply afflicted and hating my own body, not at home either in the social body, where I feel ill at ease and unfitting; not at ease at all about the body of Christ; where the whole body seems to be an anxious object full of dis-ease and unease.

But God turned to the body in Christ. Incarnation: God so loved the world that He came into it. So, too, we must consent to become incarnate for each other, to embody Love and let Love be present through us. That is the only way that people can experience it often, through our embodiment of it. Our task is to help people 'to bear the beams of Love'[11] instead of to escape from them into some terrible form of suffering.

The kind of embodied Love we need has to be as tough as old boots. It has to be able to cope with long-term testing work with people, where we have to deal with failure and betrayal and the opening of ever

---

[10] Cf. 'laughing in the mantle of variety': Jones, *Sleeping Lord*, 64.
[11] William Blake, 'The Little Black Boy', in *Poetry & Prose,* ed. Geoffrey Keynes, (London: Nonesuch, 1942), 54.

deeper wounds. With a Love of that kind, we believe theologically, because of what we know about the Gospel and about Christ, that compassion for affliction is easy. It is not.

Simone Weil says, 'It repels, rather than attracts.'[12] Deep, gaping wounds repel rather than attract. Think of some of the people you know, where others find it difficult to come near them because something pushes them away. Our deep wounds, which have been gained sometimes through shocking human relationships in the past, explode, shattering everything around them. Or they implode, and shatter the person inside. They become vehemently expressive, or withdrawnly, furiously silent. Or they become addictive, compulsive, demanding shapes, carrying a great deal of victim power, and making absolutist demands. That's what all our wounds do. The terrible wounds of the afflicted with whom we work awaken our wounds, our unmet needs, the things that have gone wrong for us too, so that we have to learn to look to our own knowledge, our own healing, in order to be able to stay close to the deep wounds of the really afflicted. And we have to learn what it means to 'wait on God'.

## Bridge Builders

All that has to make us, in the body of Christ, bridgebuilders, trying to make bridges between oneself and the other, where there is some dignity and respect in a held space between us.

Sometimes we feel we are building a bridge in mid-air; we are doing something, but Heaven knows what is at either end, or whether it will stand in the end. We have to go on with bridge-building in mid-air. We have to be mediators, helping people to find the gentle art of the possible, the power of the provisional, which can just moderate a bit that absolutist demand for the all, which can never be met. We have to help people find that the all is impossible, the nothing yawns, but

---

[12] Simone Weil, *Waiting on God*, trans. Emma Craufurd (London: Routledge and Kegan Paul Ltd, 1951), 63–8.

something matters. Something that arises in Love and Truth exchanged between people makes it possible to find a tiny square of ground on which to stand, instead of the abyss yawning completely.

In order to do that mediating, that bridge-building, we have to become what the French call bricoleurs scavengers, pickers-up of unconsidered trifles. People with sideways vision who can suddenly see something in the gutter that is worth picking up and using somewhere. Above all, we have to learn to live with brokenness, to know that the broken whole is still a potential whole, and that the great art of healing will always involve, this side of eternity, that brokenness taken into the body, my body, broken for you; our body, broken in terms of all that we can give to others in relationships, held in Christ's body, 'Broken for you...'

## Finding God

How do we find God in those places?

— As the Psalmist did: 'Save me, O God, for the waters are come in unto my soul. ... I am come in to the deep waters where the floods overflow me.' (Ps. 69:1–2 KJV) Borderlands are places of flooding, of denudation. We have to be able to stay there, as the Psalmist did, and call from that place to God.

— Or as Christ did in Gethsemane, where our commitment to love and suffering, no matter where it takes us, has to be part of our being drawn into the Christ Life in prayer and worship and thought. Non-triumphalist, not-knowing, un-knowing, un-feeling, un-doing, falling up-wards, as it were.

— Or as Christ did on the Cross, in the place of Godforsakenness and to find a glimpse that the place of Godforsakenness is the place where God most is. Unless we can find God there with people, God is elusive.

How to be able to stay in those places and find that? How to hold in there, in faith and in doubt, in the teeth of all the evidence to the contrary? Theology that dares to doubt, even to the place of Godforsakenness with others.

## Living with Doubt

Hillman, the psychologist, said, 'You have to be sane in order to be able to doubt.'[13] So sometimes in the absolutist situations in which we find ourselves, maybe our greatest sanity is to stay with the questions and the doubt and move towards that sense of almost God-forsakenness, if we are to retain some degree of sanity.

I think we can only do that through prayer and worship, as well as talking together, to know together Paul's 'groanings which cannot be uttered', the groanings from those dark places of suffering in the human condition. We have to learn to be silent, and to know that presence in the place of stillness where, at first, there seems to be nothing, but in the end it may prove to be God. How to wait on God, somewhere between death and resurrection.

## The Place Between

There is a poem by Pasternak (in his novel *Dr Zhivago*) in which he is talking through the lips of Mary Magdalene. He says this about that place between death and resurrection:

> *Those three days will pass*
> *But they will push me down into such emptiness*
> *That in the frightening interval*
> *I shall grow up to the Resurrection.*[14]

So often we have to wait with people in that frightening interval between death and resurrection, where the only chance of growing up, of surviving, of going on, depends on our capacity to wait in that kind of emptiness.

I think we have to guard against what I call, in a rather grandiose phrase, ontological collapse. We are working with people who use secular,

---

[13] James Hillman, *On Paranoia*, Eranos Lectures Series, 8 (Spring Publications, 1988).

[14] Boris Pasternak, *Dr Zhivago* (London: Collins & Harvill, 1958), 505.

humanistic language. But sometimes, I think, if we allow the God-dimension to fade away, something terrible begins to happen. I believe it is happening in our society a good deal of the time. If we do not allow for the divine, something about what we deny and refuse to acknowledge, collapses its weight onto the other things that are there. The weight of Love falls on human relationships, which are carrying too much and break under the strain. Or it falls on individuals, who cannot carry it all and end in despair and frustration, in woundedness.

## Being Present

This is the great question for me in our kind of work:

How do we keep carrying the divine dimension, the Beyond in the midst, in spite of all the deep and dark things we have to enter into, so that we do not bring about that state of terrifying ontological collapse, which perhaps leads to the kind of state which our society sounds as if it is in at the moment, with its materialism, and despair and nihilism just under the surface.

The other thing we have to do is to learn what the Quakers call 'to speak Truth to power'. There are times when we have to bear witness before those in power about where we are, what we have found, what we have heard, because those with whom we work often cannot do it adequately for themselves. (Please God, we help to empower them to do so whenever possible.) We have to have the courage to speak Truth to power.

We need to speak to the powerful about what is needed. I think, if we do that, we are saved from resentment, the kind of resentment that arises when people feel themselves to be helpless and powerless victims. If we get negatively obsessed with authority, with a smouldering, hostile emotional response to it, and with a mania for self-justification, and somehow get more and more embittered and detracting, trying to cut things down to size, somehow, if we learn to speak Truth to power together, something of that terrible resentment can be picked up, and we stop feeling so helpless.

Blake contrasts two ways of loving:

> Love seeketh not Itself to please,
> Nor for itself hath any care,
> But for another gives its ease,
> And builds a Heaven in Hell's despair.

There is Love incarnate, embodied in tough, truthful relationships between people. And then the other kind:

> Love seeketh only Self to please,
> To bind another to Its delight
> Joys in another's loss of ease
> And builds a Hell in Heaven's despite.[15]

Let us hope that the tragedies we have to share so often in our work help us to build under God the right kind of Love, that can be part of building a Heaven in Hell's despair, and not a Hell in Heaven's despite.

Blake is an extraordinary poet. He goes on to talk about the mysteriousness of the inter-penetration of the divine and the human, which is what theology is all about. He says:

> Tho' thou art Worship'd by the Names Divine
> Of Jesus & Jehovah, thou art still
> The Son of Morn in weary Night's decline,
> The lost Traveller's Dream under the Hill.[16]

The God who is less easily named, the God who is mysteriously there, in the borderlands that we have to share with people. Named or unnamed, God is present. Are we?

---

[15] 'The Clod and the Pebble', in Blake, *Poetry & Prose*, 66.
[16] Epilogue to 'The Gates of Paradise', in Blake, *Poetry & Prose*, 579.

# Sounding Stones: Reflections on the Mystery of the Feminine

## Introduction

I want to try to evoke and resonate certain qualities in our life together as women to see if it meets anything in you. I spend a lot of time in my work as a psychotherapist listening to other women sharing their lives with me, often women who are living and working together—sometimes religious, sometimes other people. I take a staff support group at Sobell House for the dying, here in Oxford, and quite a few of them come to talk to me too. Some of their problems are about what it means to work together as a group of women and what issues are specifically connected with that. I think there is a call at work, a call of the Spirit in the Church for us to try to work together to see what we can find.

In talking to you here I am going to assume certain things that are basic to my thinking about this subject, which in other contexts—where people might not have such a firm Christian background—I would go into in detail. Because I can assume that Christian imagery is a living factor for you I may say more in a psychological vein than I might otherwise. Were I discussing my understanding of the feminine and feminine ways to God with another group, the emphasis would be different. I would develop these assumptions and draw on the scriptural and liturgical traditions about, for example, the Mother of God, to identify and express my understanding of the mystery of the feminine. The tradition of the Church can nourish our own experience of Annunciation, of what we mean by virginity, of bearing and gestating, of Visitation, of bringing to birth and nurturing, and of living with the element of passion in our natures. That would be one way of approaching our subject, and in a way is contained in it, but today I want to do something different.

So many things connected with the feminine and women are not capable of direct statement, so although there is form to this talk it is not the form of rational development—though I hope it will be reasonably rational! I am going to use some stones (collected mostly in the north of England and on Mull and Iona) as markers for thoughts around a theme. It's not easy to find words. In the centre I am going to put this stone with a hole in the middle which speaks of the mystery of the feminine, about something silent to which we must be able to hold, and I want to build the other stones round it in a circle. So don't try to relate them to each other, just try to take each one and see if it relates to the basic theme for you.

## Laughing in the Mantle of Variety

> *mother of particular perfections*
> *queen of otherness*
> *mistress of asymmetry*
>
> *patroness of things counter, parti, pied, several*
> *protectress of things known and handled*
> *help of things familiar and small*
>     *wardress of the secret crevices*
>     *of things wrapped and hidden …*
>   *arc of differences*
>   *tower of individuation*
>   *queen of the minivers*
> *laughing in the mantle of variety …*

David Jones, *The Sleeping Lord*

That seems to me among other things to be a beautiful prayer to the Mother of God and what she stands for in our tradition, but also something about our feminine need to hold to the 'holy diversities'. It reminds us that traditionally it is always said that the feminine is 'most particular', with play on that phrase: dealing with particulars, in small things, in things that matter, that make all the difference; and yet on the shadow side, the pernickety bitchiness that's most particular, too particular, too much after each other's guts when something starts going wrong. We must rejoice in being collectors of bits and pieces. I think the large inescapable truths are not easily come by in our day and generation, in a time of cultural fragmentation, and the truth, amongst us in the Christian Church too, has to be found in bits and pieces, and treasured in the heart when we find it. Truth will often lie in small things, the things that come in the dark, the things that need gestating in order for them to grow at all. In our drawing to the contemplative life we need to be able to do that for the Church: to restate, to cherish, to treasure, to ponder the small things that are given, on behalf of the Church as a whole.

Now that means that we have to try to learn not to generalize, not to universalize, too soon. We need the 'logos capacity', often associated with the masculine, which does generalize, does universalize, but we do it at the risk of losing our own sense of the particular. We have to hold to not leaving things out of account. If we give birth too quickly to the truth as it begins to emerge, it comes out as ideology and as ideas that we wish to impose on each other, not as something that is generative, that comes to birth, that has form and meaning amongst us.

The other thing I think we have to try not to do is to assimilate or domesticate the truth too much. As women we sometimes have a tendency to want to tame things, to make them domesticated and familiar—and that's a good capacity, but we can go too far. Truths which are large and fierce and not easily approached are turned into tame pussy-cats. They are not! They need to keep their tiger quality.

## Marrying Logos and Eros

When we talk about our experience together as women, we often find that there is some kind of tension between love and truth—can we both learn to live together in love and yet learn to live and tell the truth? This is a question about taking seriously both the masculine and feminine components of our selves. For the sake of argument—and it does, of course, need arguing—I am calling the masculine in us the 'logos capacity', and the feminine (the capacity for sheer relatedness, the desire for love and so forth) 'eros'. It means taking seriously what Jung calls our 'animus problem', the male inside me, the male inside you—and what we can do about it.

It is sometimes said that a woman can use her animus as either a light or a knife. Either we can take our capacity for clarity and perception and stick it into someone so that they collapse (we are particularly good at sticking someone in the back), or we can use it as a luminous quality, something held in connection with the feminine and our deeper wisdom, so that people can find their own way forward in the light it provides—and we can too. I think that a good deal of what you do in *lectio divina* is about a way of thinking which marries the logos and eros. We let them work together somewhere inside us. André Louf in his book *Teach Us to Pray*[1] has written about 'rocking and chewing the word'—now here are both the feminine images, 'rocking and chewing', the repetitive things, and the word, *logos spermatikos*, the generative word.

We have to learn to recognize the logos and give it some form in our lives. This involves being able to employ our talents creatively. I know the tradition in the contemplative life says we must yield our talents, and that is also true. Nevertheless, if people are not using their logos capacity it becomes, as it were, overwrought: it walks round and round inside us like a tiger in a cage, snarling to itself, occasionally lashing its claws and swiping at somebody through the bars. The Jungians say, if a woman is in that state, 'Put the animus to work: give it a task, give it direction, give it motivation, a sense of purpose, of clarity of some kind—it must be done!' That can help when everything is going round and round inside.

Marrying logos and eros also involves relating to actual men who come our way, the other half of the universe. Often it is the case that men find it difficult to 'take a woman neat': they are not always sure what to do with a woman's strength. They can take our weakness, they can take our vulnerability, they can certainly take our obedience and our submission, our general anxiety to please and to conform, but often they do find it difficult to take us 'concentrated'. And we have to learn

---

[1] André Louf, *Teach Us to Pray*, trans. Hubert Hoskins (London: Darton, Longman and Todd, 1974).

both to know our own strength and to allow for it in relationships. Many women now despise what used to be called 'women's wiles'. They think it is a kind of game-playing and something we should not do; but maybe it is also something of the stuff of which the universe is made: we have to be not only as gentle as doves but as wise as serpents—not in a deceitful and underhand way, but just learning how to make life possible for those around us, including the men. If we don't, what happens, especially in the women's movement, is that we make the men impotent. They feel castrated, they feel they have nothing to offer, they don't know what to do with themselves any more. If life is difficult for women in today's world, it is even more difficult for men— they don't know what to do about what is happening to the women. If we want impotent men, well, we are fools.

## Fostering the Capacity to be Alone

I know that there is great emphasis in your life on the need to be alone with God, and that there are times in the lives of many of you when that is more, or sometimes less, easy to do. I want to talk about it a little from a psychological point of view because it links very much with the kind of work a therapist does with people. A good deal of therapy is, in the end, helping a person to be alone in the presence of the therapist.

How difficult or easy is it for us genuinely to be alone? The answer will be different for each of us. Do we enjoy solitude when we have it? Certainly we long for it and wish that we were given more time for it, but what happens when we have it? Are we capable of enjoying it, making use of it, finding it creative? or, in fact, when we have it do we not often begin to feel persecuted, threatened, anxious, overwhelmed by the experience? Now it is believed in developmental psychological theory that a child first learns a capacity to be alone by learning it in the presence of another. It is something that is part of a relationship. Picture a child absorbed in play with the mother or father there in the same room, but not unduly anxious, not interfering or keeping up a conversation with the child all the time, letting him be.

The child feels safe. The protective presence of the parent supports the child's fragile but growing ego. And this experience becomes part of the child's inner world, so that later in life somewhere inside there is a sense of a benign presence which protects one's frailty when faced with aloneness. This is the stuff out of which friendship is made — friendship which is not driven by need or desire but is able to enjoy the company of the other without undue stress or strain or exchange, which can take silence. It is one of these terrible, awful mysteries that it is very difficult for people who have not known that benign presence of a parent in early life to feel God as a benign presence. They believe it in their minds but they don't experience it in their guts and on their nerve-endings when they are in their aloneness. It seems to me that here we can help each other, we can help each other to have that experience of being alone in the presence of another. I think that happens in your life here. Some of my own longing and capacity for being silent and alone, and my desire to start a prayer group which could offer that kind of experience of being alone with God with others in silence, came through my experience of praying in your chapel here. It has contributed to my appreciation of other people's need for that experience too.

To be alone does mean struggling and working with the negative, hostile, critical, threatening and anxious bits inside us. There is no way round it. When I look back to my own childhood I can certainly see images of the black side as well as the light side of it. No matter how good the parenting one is still aware of 'the child crying in the night with no language but a cry'.[2] But from my childhood I also remember my mother singing somewhere behind me in the house while I played outside on the doorstep. She had a beautiful soaring soprano voice of the kind that always reaches the top notes without difficulty. It was the benign presence to set over against 'the child crying in the night'.

---

[2] 'In Memoriam A. H. H. OBIIT MDCCCXXXIII: 54', in Alfred, Lord Tennyson, *In Memoriam* (London: E. Moxon, 1850).

## Stalking our Wildness

By 'stalking our wildness' we try to allow in our life together for that bit inside us which isn't fitting in, for what isn't on the way to sanctity but is somewhere a bit wilder than that! Many women are looking at this and, strangely, it brings them in touch with what chastity in the religious life means, what an essential virginity or integrity of soul means. In terms of Greek mythology this is 'the Artemis quality'. You will remember that Artemis was the one who was wild, pure, unsullied and untouched nature. She keeps us in touch with the high places and the distant places, with our need for the mountains and the hills, as it were, where we can run and be alone. We need to be in touch with the uncanny, with the numinous, with the bits that aren't domesticated or brought very easily into the common life. Artemis stands for our capacity for solitude, for reserve, for having something in reserve, not living it all 'up front'. Many communities at the moment who are concerned with running their community life only in human relationship terms, with constant exchanges about what people are feeling and thinking, have got it all a bit 'up front' I think.

Stalking our wildness also means finding the bits in us that are vulnerable. One of the stories about Artemis is that she could not bear a man to take her by surprise, to come upon her naked, unexpectedly. It is finding that part in us that needs a certain reserve, integrity, to bear our own vulnerability. But we have to be aware too that Artemis was capable of being wild to the point of gruesomeness, and cruel to the point of repulsiveness; that side of us must learn to take its own hardness and disdainfulness into account. We have to take the negative face of the virgin seriously, the virago aspect, the cold, high, cruel, isolated side that there can be to chastity, which leads eventually, in other spheres, to sterility. I have known it to lead in the religious life to symptoms of vertigo, dizziness, eye-trouble. Often the images which arise when we explore it are something to do with being too high, with the feeling that you are going to fall, that you have to fall—and that is the answer to it, you are too high up somewhere, you have to come down to earth. So we need to be able to both stalk our wildness and to be able to deal with it if it takes us somewhere too far out and up.

## Making Sure We Are Earthed

In nineteenth-century novels women are often described by men as 'good earth'—many women today don't think much of that expression! For a man something in the feminine picks up his alter ego, is a mirror for his soul, picking up the earth and cosmos for him. We are crazy if we try to yield that completely and say it doesn't matter to us. When that happens it seems to me that instead of running 'a good earth policy' we are running 'a scorched earth policy', and that really is a form of madness in our life together as women. We need at times to be able to go back to earth, to find the dark places where we can hide and snarl a bit if we are to find deeper healing. We need to keep in touch with cooking and gardening, and with the rhythms of the body, of the womb-rhythms which enter into the traditional pursuits of women, rocking, spinning, weaving, waiting and the forms which they might take in modern life (which are not always easy to find, come to that). We need repeating, cyclic, rhythmic, ritualistic ways and occupations that can keep us in touch with earth and the deeper cyclic rhythms of the feminine. Otherwise we become like the 'handless maiden' in the Grimm fairy tale—out of touch.

Hestia, another Greek goddess, was the keeper of the hearth. We need to find that part within us which can feed that tiny flame which might still be there somewhere at the centre of our being. If only we can just keep it alight, make a place of warmth! Cold is a killer—Fr Gilbert recognized that cold is a killer spiritually speaking, for you cannot pray when you are too cold. Hell is cold, not hot. When we get too cold and miserable we need to make a place of warmth, to find the cat or a hot-water bottle or something, to do for ourselves what we would do in other spheres, for our children or our husbands when they are sick or in need. That capacity is an important part of our life together—feeding the flame slowly, gently, in order not to quench it. And, in the Church, being guardians of myth and memory is part of making sure that we are earthed and centred.

## *Discovering the Creative* No

There is a Native American myth which says that Man and Woman were seen standing on the top of the universe, praying to God. The man was standing with his arms raised and open in an attitude of invocation, saying the creative Yes to God. And the woman was standing with her arms held downwards, saying the creative No to God. There is a strange paradox there. It is as if the man needs to learn to open himself to his vulnerability, to relationship, to learn to say the Yes; and something inside us as women which lives in that basic relatedness, needs to be able to say the *No* in order to let the other be, to save the other from feeling smothered or too tightly bound in our feminine need to give and to love.

Our essential self as women includes our capacity for relatedness, and wounds to that relatedness are wounds to our very self. But they are necessary wounds. We must learn to bear them and to bear with them; they are the kind of wounds that are both wound (*blessure* is the old word) and blessing. The link between wound and blessing is very close. If we are to open ourselves to the other as separate from us, and not just an extension of our ego or the object of our need to give and to love, then we have to be able to take the wounds to our relatedness which go deeper than anything else.

We want to love and to be loved. Many women say to me that although they are not so physically, psychologically, they are whores —they will do anything for love. That is deeply part of our nature, we will do anything for love. But we have to be able to yield that need if we are to be able to find the deeper ways of being with the other. That means learning to say No to our selves. It's a work against nature on behalf of transformed nature, part of the Gospel, it seems to me. We have to bear and to suffer aloneness and woundedness in order to allow the other to be. We have to learn to say No in our capacity as mothers so that the child may become independent, may separate from us, be weaned. We have to say No to our profound desire to comfort, alleviate, console, so that we may learn what the 'foot of the Cross' presence with the Beloved in suffering means.

## How to be Near and Far at the Same Time

In relationships two capacities are necessary, the capacity to be near and the capacity to be far. We all have capacities in us which draw us towards, make us long for, union, unity—with the other and ultimately with God. But we can only find the deeper meaning of that yearning if we take seriously our need to be just who we are, individuals, created as separate, yet made for relationship. We need to be able to manage both distance and nearness. Most of us find that one or other of those things is easier. We have to try to develop in ourselves, spiritually as well as psychologically, the capacity for the one we are bad at.

I want to talk about the place of anger as part of that process. We all know a great deal about the kind of tenderness, gentleness, longing for, the other, that can bring us to intimacy and nearness. But what about learning to stand apart as individuals in order to step into relatedness more deeply? One of the things, again, that we can learn from early childhood is that the child learns its independence from the mother, its capacity for distance, by its use of exploratory anger— temper tantrums, the burst of energy which says 'Keep away from me! I must have what I want! Anger has a sort of survival value to us in teaching us independence and weaning us from over-clinging dependency on people. Anger in that sense is a separating energy, which is the other side of that uniting energy which draws us together. We need to be able to use as a pulse both the energies which draw us together and the ones which pull us apart.

It is not always easy to express that kind of separating energy; it is what words are given us for, I think, to explore our differences as well as our samenesses. We need the capacity to assert, to dare to be who we are. So many of us, in the end, lack the courage to be. The lives of so many people, of those who suffer from depression, are an apology for existence. They cannot accept a strong doctrine of creation which says that God makes us and looks on us and sees that it is *good*—despite all the things which may be wrong and need to be dealt with.

The trouble is that in our life together anger gets masked; we need to recognize some of those masks. First of all, compliance: we can mask anger by conformity, by an extra effort to fit in and be nice, kind, clean, good Sisters. That compliance is not very deep; it is a surface defence masking deeper feelings. Or we can be chronic appeasers, anxious to please—but just underneath there is a certain whining, moaning, nagging quality which too often surfaces when things go wrong. Or another mask is submission. Religious life teaches us a great deal about submission, but if submission leads to repression merely pushing down, rather than a process of transformation, then we get outbursts and eruptions, and doors banging! These eruptions are difficult to deal with, they are destructive when they happen, but they happen because we haven't learnt how to stage a fair fight somewhere in our life together, to allow an arena where differences can be explored and owned and looked at. Another mask is general irritability, always feeling a bit out of sorts with ourselves and with the environment. No one is ever pleased or really suited on those sorts of days. Another mask is a kind of clinging which conceals the anxiety, the anxious dependency, on the other. We are afraid that if our aggressive thoughts or feelings got out the relationship would be lost, so we cling. And again, some people use as a mask an aggressive, teasing humour. Now that can be marvellous and lighten the atmosphere, but it can also be a way of continually putting down the other.

We have to be able to look at these things and then decide whether it might not be better to learn how to stage a fair fight. There are processes—of discussion, of admission, of allowing for the fact that someone may say one thing fiercely now, but having said it may go away for twenty-four hours and be feeling quite different by tomorrow.

Sometimes we do indeed want to be difficult and to destroy, but often too we long for reconciliation, we long for the relationship to be restored. It is as real an urge in us as in the other. If only we can allow for the way in which a person's mind can change, if only we can allow the feelings expression, then something much more real can happen in our life together. So often in our swift and speedy age we make decisions that are based on what we say now, at this moment in a discussion, and do not take into account the long natural processes of the emotional life. The mind is quick, the emotions are slow and they have to go through various transformations. We do know something of these transformations, of the process of forgiveness, which we often try to do too quickly. Things may be repressed and banked up underneath; we do not sufficiently allow for the long term processes of forgiveness. Emotional processes, their natural and transformational history take time—we must learn to make time for them in our life together.

I said at the beginning that I would be taking our Christian commitment and the centrality of Christian images for us, for granted. But, finally, I want all that I have said to 'sound together' in the presence of Christ, that Presence which 'makes all the difference' to our experience. I want to share with you that sense of distance and nearness which is held for us in our knowledge of Christ in our life together, which speaks to us both of the aloneness and the essential character of being in relationship. In *Waiting on God*, Simone Weil is writing of the Passion; she says that the glorified body of Christ bore the marks of the nails and the spear, the 'necessary wounds':

> God created through love and for love. God did not create anything except love itself, and the means to love. He created love in all its forms. He created beings capable of love from all possible distances. Because no other could do it, he himself went to the greatest possible distance, the infinite distance. This infinite distance between God and God, this supreme tearing apart, this agony beyond all others, this marvel of love is the crucifixion ...
>
> This tearing apart, over which supreme love places the bond of supreme union, echoes perpetually across the universe in the midst of

the silence, like two notes, separate yet melting into one, like pure and heart-rending harmony. This is the Word of God. The whole creation is nothing but its vibration. When human music in its greatest purity pierces our soul, this is what we hear through it. When we have learnt to hear the silence, this is what we grasp more distinctly through it.[3]

---

[3] Simone Weil, *Waiting on God*, trans. Emma Craufurd (London: Routledge and Kegan Paul Ltd, 1951), 68.

# Exploring Silence

## ABOUT THE ICON OF THE 'PERFECT' SILENCE

The form of this icon first appeared in sixteenth-century Russia. Sometimes called 'Our Saviour of the Blessed Silence', it is an image, or icon, of the 'perfect' silence shown to us by Christ, revealing to us the One whom we seek in contemplative, monastic, ascetic, silent prayer. It helps us to quieten our spirit and deepen the prayer of silence before God.

The Messiah is shown as a winged youth in royal robes with hands crossed, and without the usual book or scroll. He is the Angel of God's Presence[1] and is linked with the passage:

---

[1] Cf. Is. 63:9 (NKJV).

The Spirit of wisdom and understanding,
The Spirit of counsel and might,
The Spirit of knowledge and of the fear of the LORD. (Is. 11:2)

The halo reveals that it is a messianic Christ icon. The Cross of the Resurrected Christ's victory over death is shown in the halo. The Incarnation is shown in the superimposed quadrilaterals. The dark blue [here black] represents heaven, and the red represents earth: the two natures of Christ in one Person. The fourth corner of the 'heavenly' quadrilateral is hidden, the eighth corner of the whole. It represents the Eighth Day, known only by the Father, not by human beings or angels.

Silence is shown in the crossed hands of receptive non-action; in the general portrayal of patience and long-suffering, gifts of the Spirit; and in an atmosphere of blessed silence. The icon draws us into the silence, calls us to deepen our silent prayer in Christ, and leaves us with the awesome responsibility of our created freedom to choose and to follow in joyful assent and in times of affliction: '... he was afflicted, yet he did not open his mouth' (Is. 53:7).

We long for Christ's 'coming again'. Here we see how to wait in that longing, in the deep silence of prayerful waiting upon God.

[The illustration opposite is of the author's *Icon of the 'Perfect' Silence* given to her by the icon writer, Militza Zernov. Ed.]

# Introduction

I notice with a feeling of wry recognition that Abba Agatho, when he first went into the desert, kept a stone in his mouth for three years, until he learnt to be silent. And here I am, struggling with words about silence. I must say what I can, and then go out and look for that stone!

To every opening line of the children's song, 'I like peace, I like quiet', my three sons used, when they were young, to reply rumbustiously, in word and deed, 'I like noise, I like riot'. Small wonder, then, that I am attracted to silence. Certainly I have found for a number of years that exploring silence in the context of the Christian tradition and the sacramental life is what gives my activity meaning.

One of my favourite stories is drawn from family life. It is the one about a mother who, against her better judgement, was showing her children an old-fashioned illustrated book of Christian stories. One picture was a particularly gruesome one of Christians being thrown to the lions. The mother was dismayed to see her three-year-old in tears. 'Oh dear', she said, 'what is the matter?' To which the child replied, 'Oh mummy, look, that poor little lion hasn't got a Christian.' This story seems to illustrate some of the necessary attitudes in any approach to prayer: that we should have a certain flexibility of expectation, and that we should be careful not to generalise about what other people may be experiencing. Don't do unto others as you would be done by, because others are different—as the proverb does not say. There are many ways of approach. What suits one might be quite wrong for another, and what works for us at one stage in our life might not always work. We need to be as flexible and open to the Holy Spirit as possible, without overlooking at the same time a need for the rhythm of habit and tradition and regularity. Prayer seems to me both an art, open to the deepest creative impulses in our being, and a discipline involving rhythm, accepting the systole and diastole, the ebb and flow. Sometimes I need patiently to relax and allow things to happen, so that I can, as it were, see the space between the bars. At other times I need to find a framework, something upon which I can lean when times are bad; and equally, when a Pentecostal experience breaks through the old patterns and needs a deeper integration, there is the need to discover a new form.

Of one thing I am sure: that I find it easier to talk *to* God than I do to talk *about* God, and I know that I am not alone in this. The words no longer seem quite to fit for many people. We must take heart from a favourite saying of Eastern Orthodox Christians, 'The one who prays is a theologian, and the theologian is one who prays.' The living commitment to God is the first step in understanding. Between the *kerygma* (what is revealed in the Bible, Church and Tradition) and our existence (our daily experience in this century) falls a shadow. Many are finding that the old formulations are slipping from them and, in the words of Stevie Smith's poem,

> I was much too far out all my life
> And not waving but drowning.[2]

The image that often recurs in my mind is of myself climbing a familiar flight of stairs. A sudden stumble makes me reach out for support—only to find that the banisters are no longer there. Words without banisters. Are we then condemned to lives of quiet despair? I find help in the title of Fritz Schumacher's brilliant book *Small is Beautiful*. We must be prepared to start small from where we are, and not pine away with striving after the unattainable. We must stop struggling with words and meanings and restore a balance, spending more time exploring the silence from which words come.

## Approaching Silence

In a small way I have begun to find that the seeking of an inner silence in prayer provides a way which can sometimes heal and unite bits of me that seem a long way from each other. So much of our experience

---

[2] The poem 'Not Waving but Drowning', in Stevie Smith, *Selected Poems*, ed. James MacGibbon (Penguin, 1978), 167, has been widely anthologized.

in life is tacit; words are only one means of communication. If words fail, let us look at other means and keep quiet until we find we have something to say. In some mysterious way, I think that what begins to happen is that not only do we begin to explore silence, but silence begins to explore us.

We are all battered by the noise and intrusiveness of our external environment, not only in terms of physical noise, but also in the assault on our capacity for sensitive concern, by all the sociological and psychological analysis, by the flow of televisual information and by ecological outrage. I think many of us are aware as never before of a need to counterbalance all this by being able to find an internal centre of gravity in the indwelling Christ, an inner fulcrum which might lift the world for us into the light of the eternal. We feel an urge to explore the possibilities of inner space, space which we sense must match in its vastness and mystery the images brought back by astronauts.

There are, of course, on all journeys in strange places, times when I panic and wish I'd never come—times when I'm sure that I've lost my passport, that I haven't acquired the necessary visas, and above all that I don't know the language and cannot communicate. I am suddenly vulnerable, exposed, dependent on finding someone to help, at the mercy of the 'unknown'. Yet for Christians the unknown is God himself. 'We are all in him enclosed', as Mother Julian says. Wherever the journey takes me, I cannot be taken out of God, provided I commit myself to God in faith, hope and love—even if the ways in which he leads me seem very strange to my understanding. If I find myself in dry deserts, or on vast, heaving oceans, or in the worst hells of the human mind, or just struggling on with my suburban existence, God is there. God promises that the Holy Spirit will never be refused as a source of inner strength to those who ask. I must ask and ask for a growing life in the Spirit until I can say with Job, 'though he slay me, yet will I trust in him' (Job 13:15 NKJV). Always, however obscure to our eyes, there is around us and in us the possibility of joy in the vast 'more' of the Unknown—God himself—and the possibility of living a life of faith and trust in God.

## *Allowing Things to Happen*

Once upon a time a village in China was suffering under a famine. The villagers had tried long and hard to produce rain by magic, witchcraft and ritual. At last they sent for a rainmaker from a distant village. In a few days a quiet little old man appeared. He settled down in a hut; he did what jobs needed to be done in and around the hut. And in three days the rain came. Sometimes all we can do in an intolerable situation is quietly to do the next thing, wait and allow things to happen—to be the kind of person around whom things *can* happen. (I admit that I do not always find it easy to distinguish between a wise passivity and my inveterate laziness and inertia, but the distinction needs to be made.)

In a book by the Jewish philosopher Martin Buber entitled *A Believing Humanism: Gleanings,*[3] there is a poem about Elijah. Buber uses the biblical events as images of Elijah's various states of mind as a prophet. Elijah would like to be a wind, blasting, blowing, stirring up:

> You sought me on your stormy paths,
> And did not find me.

He would like to have been a prophetic fire, burning, scorching and kindling:

> You sought Me in your flaming abysses
> And did not find Me.

It was not until he was overcome by silence, bowed to the earth in despair, that he became aware of deeper levels of his being and could allow things to happen, and then heard the voice of God in 'the hovering silence'.

An entry for 14 June 1843 in her journal by the Quaker Caroline Fox, reads:

> It is the fuss and bustle principle which must proclaim itself until it
> is hoarse, that wars against Truth and Heroism. Let Truth be done in

---

[3] Martin Buber, *A Believing Humanism: Gleanings* (London and New York: Simon & Schuster, 1969), 37.

silence till it is forced to speak, and then, should it only whisper, all those whom it may concern will hear.[4]


## Being Present Where We Are

One of the Jewish Hasidic tales is about Rabbi Isaac son of Yekel who lived in Kraków. He had a dream that under the pillar of a certain bridge in Prague treasure was to be found. So off he went to look for it. After he had been skulking about looking for an opportunity to dig, the guard on the bridge asked him what he was doing. Eventually he told him. The guard roared with laughter and said, 'Why, you silly man, you shouldn't take any notice of dreams. Only the other night I dreamt that in Cracow there was treasure hidden under the house of a Rabbi Isaac son of Yekel. Why, as you know, every second Rabbi is an Isaac son of Yekel'. But Rabbi Isaac son of Yekel went home.

God meets us where we are, and not where we are not, or when we are only half there. God dwells where we let him in. In another Hasidic tale the Rabbi Zusya said, 'At the end I shall be asked, not, "Why were you not Moses?" but, "Why were you not Zusya?"'

We have to start with God where we are and as we are, and perhaps the difficulty which we all have in doing this can be the pivot that will enable us to 'turn' to God. I like the Hebrew word which Martin Buber loved to use, *teshuva*, meaning 'turning'—a strong and concrete physical image, the origin of our later ideas of repentance and penitence. The important thing is not what we feel but the fact that we turn to God and realise that there is always the possibility of transforming a situation through the 'turning'. At the very least it can turn bottomless despair into positive compunction, which can look up and out. A Rabbi was once asked, 'Why can we no longer hear the Word of God?' and the Rabbi answered, 'Because we can no longer stoop low enough to hear God's voice.'

---

[4] See *The Journals of Caroline Fox, 1835–1871: A Selection*, ed. Wendy Monk (London: Paul Elek, 1972).

## Entering into Silence

Those of us who, in total dependence on the Holy Spirit, are seeking the contemplative way in the midst of a busy and unpredictable life, have to face the fact that the initial stages of 'tuning in' to silence are often very difficult. How can I cut through the constant pressure of my internal chatter into something deeper? We all have to experiment with various aids to find out which of them are most helpful to us. In these days of yoga, relaxation and psycho-prophylactic methods of childbirth, there is hardly need to mention that deep breathing and good posture can help — and are acquired only through teaching and practice.

I suspect that most of us find one of our senses more dominant than the others. If we can find a way of concentrating that one, then the rest will be held in check with it. For someone whose visual sense is strong it may help to let their eyes dwell on an icon or a crucifix, or on some symbol that holds the contradictions of life and its mysteries, and allow the truths they reveal to mediate themselves to us while we concentrate our attention gently on them, treating them as a window on to truth. Others find that reading for a while can help, using the words as a sort of 'audile icon' through which they can listen and hear the truth coming to them. I myself am what is known as a 'haptic' type (enjoying form with the implied sense of touch, as in sculpture); so I find that if I am feeling disintegrated I can concentrate myself best by best by running the knots in a piece of wool or string through my fingers, feeling the shape of each knot firmly and linking it with the repetition of a prayer or phrase. This is of course the rosary method, the 'Rose-garden Game' so well described in a book of that name by Eithne Wilkins.[5] Experience has convinced me that we must be open to new possibilities of ways in which the senses can lead us into silence and meaning. I remember once going to an exhibition of kinetics (works of art that make their impact through movement). I was admiring three forms that were

[5] Eithne Wilkins, *The Rose-Garden Game. The Symbolic Background to the European Prayer-Beads* (London: Victor Gollancz, 1969).

standing still, close to each other, when someone pressed the button that set them in action. Suddenly I was oceans deep in the Trinity — three static forms became a unity through movement and interaction. Most of our models of the universe and of human behaviour are now dynamic, not static, and are governed by researches into communication and interaction. They often seem to me to present us with very vivid symbols for the divine activity and its interaction with the dynamics of human life.

I think for me it has been the gradual discovery of how to concentrate the faculties quietly through a dominant sense that has proved a way of pulling thought, feeling and straying intuitions together so that I can begin, in the Quaker phrase, to 'centre down' and listen, look, stretch towards that which is beyond, in the silence.

There are times, of course, when one emotion is so dominant that I am drowned in it: an anxiety obsesses me; a depression darkens me; a joy unearths me. It is no good fighting with these states—the more I scold myself, the more stubborn they become. If the mood cannot be ignored then it has to be released, explored, opened out before God, not left travelling round the confines of my ego. This can be a difficult, painfully prolonged business if certain moods or states of mind simply do not shift. There may be something we cannot see for ourselves which is producing this state of mind. Perhaps one mood is masking another that we don't want to know about (for example, depression masking aggression, anxious conformity masking rebelliousness). We have to be sensible and recognise the times when we need to go to someone for help, or ask for their prayers. And if there does not seem to be anyone, then we must ask God to send someone. And God does.

I recognize that for those who are much more capable of pure thought than I am, there are times when thought must be pursued to its limit and held there in a state of balanced tension—the state that Simone Weil explores in her concept of *attente de Dieu*, waiting on God.

All of us know what it is to be tired, exhausted, grey with weariness, and at those times too we must allow ourselves, without strain, just to be like that, in the presence of God who knows and cares. After all, I am no less God's child asleep than awake. René Voillaume, in *Seeds of the Desert: Legacy of Charles de Foucauld*, describes what a real experience the prayer of tiredness has to become for the Little Brothers and Sisters of Jesus in the way they have chosen.[6] Perhaps our tiredness and weariness can be an offering we make to God for all the tiredness and weariness of our world, the sharing in prayer of the burdens of others who may know no source of strength.

Perhaps one of the more useful divisions of the world is that between introversion and extroversion. People do seem to vary between those who can most easily achieve a measure of silence by shutting their eyes and looking within and those whose best hope lies in focussing on an object outside themselves. Perhaps the introverted person, who has an active inner life, finds it easier to still the mind by looking away to the outside. Equally, the extrovert needs to look in, away from the excitement of external stimuli.

In regard to actual interruptions from outside, the most helpful attitude I have found occurs in one of the stories of the Desert Fathers. A man came and stayed with a hermit and apologised as he left for breaking in on the hermit's rule of life. The hermit replied, 'My rule is to receive you with hospitality and to let you go in peace.' Not all my friends would appreciate my phrasing it quite like that, but I take the point.

In his *A Pilgrim's Book of Prayers* Fr Gilbert Shaw provides a good summary of our attempts to enter into silence:

> The soul is inspired, instructed, and supported by the Holy Spirit, but its operations and knowledge are carried out and gained through the ordinary channels of its natural faculties. It must therefore use the powers which God has given it of perception, memory, understanding, emotional feeling, and imagination, so as to bring into activity its will to depend on God.[7]

---

[6] René Voillaume, *Seeds of the Desert: The Legacy of Charles de Foucauld* (London: Anthony Clarke Books, 1972).

[7] Gilbert Shaw, *A Pilgrim's Book of Prayers* (SLG Press, 1992), Intro. p. xii.

Whatever preliminary exercises I may find helpful, they are not an end in themselves, or ways of expanding my consciousness (though they may do so), but means towards establishing a unity of my being Godwards, of being at the disposal of God's presence, of being able to listen and to hear.

## The Eternal Listener in Silence

In the Christian tradition silence is more often associated with the image of a listening companion than with a place emptied of sound. Learning to listen more to God is not, I suspect, very different from learning to listen more to my friends and neighbours. We probably all have to admit to sharing at times the tendency of the American writer and cartoonist James Thurber (1894–1961) not to listen when anybody else is talking, preferring to keep our mind a blank until they have finished and we can talk ourselves. Even more I recognize in myself the way in which a Scottish friend of ours says, 'I hear you, I hear you', when he means that he hears all right but does not intend to budge one inch in response.

Perhaps one could suggest several ways in which we might learn to listen to others. We can listen with a quality of relaxed attentiveness, so that the other knows that we are 'there' and yet not imposing our re-actions too soon on whatever he or she may want to explore with us. Many things only take an actual shape for us in the atmosphere of trust provided by someone who really can and will listen. We can listen to what is said—to what is actually given, open and apparent between us in the situation—and respond with all that we are and can appropri-ately give at that moment; leaving the other free, and yet confirmed in their existence and potentiality. We can try to listen to what is *not* being said—what is being left out, hidden, kept back, not yet formulated—perhaps because there is not yet enough trust in our presence in the situation to allow certain things to be said. We must respond to that, too, with all the tacit sensitivity we have, in an enabling way, respecting to the uttermost the secrets and privacy of the other. Sometimes, too, we need to listen to the relationship itself, to what is going on at a deeper level between this 'other' and me. Are we using each other as objects rather than as real people? Are we getting at each other in some subtle, power-driven or masochistic way, so that we are very far from genuine encounter of the kind described so beautifully in a phrase of Rilke: 'Two solitudes that protect, touch and greet one another'? Then, also, from the deepest layers of our being, we can seek to listen to the beyond, the 'more', to that which is not yet immanent—we can listen towards the will of God.

I remember how my life was transformed during my professional training as a psychiatric social worker, when I realised how, by using words of exploration rather than of definition, one could open up new worlds of listening, learning and being, and create, as it were, a space in a relationship in which both people concerned could find more freedom to be, to express themselves, could have room to manoeuvre. In the context of listening, 'I wonder' seems to me a more creative phrase than 'I think' or 'I know'; so does the phrasing of thoughts as questions rather than as blunt statements which can force the other person into the position of having to reject or accept instead of being free to go on exploring. We all know that when we are feeling low and vulnerable, a rejection of what we say can feel very much like a rejection of us. Because they are grateful for our involvement, it is sometimes very difficult for persons who are dependent on us (however momentarily) as a listener to their problems, to reject outright something we say. How many of us have found ourselves in false situations in this way! We should always try to open a window rather than slam a door when we are called upon to listen very hard to someone in need. When we think of the tenderness and freedom God allows us, can we allow less to each other?

Beyond, beneath, within all our listening is the presence of the Eternal Listener, sustaining and enabling, listening in (and to) depths we shall never exhaust or fathom. This is no less true of our listening in prayer than of our listening to another human being.

## *Sifting Silence*

I have said that it is sometimes silence that seems to explore us, to 'sift us', as the old Quakers used to say. There was said to be a strange sifting power in George Fox's silences. Once, for instance, he met with followers, testers and detractors in the country—and kept them for three hours while he sat in silence on a haystack. And they waited.

The silence sifts us because when we leave time and space in order to face what is inside us, we find out things we do not want to know. We have to learn to discover that things are different from what we thought; we might find, like the women after the Resurrection, the grave of our hopes empty and our true hope risen elsewhere, in a place in which we were not accustomed to look.

As a British art critic said of the women depicted in the cartoons of James Thurber: 'Inside every Little Nell there lurks a Lady Macbeth.' We have to learn to accept Lady Macbeth and find out how to live with her, neither letting her take control nor keeping her so repressed that she can only act secretly, as a saboteuse, poisoner and destroyer of what we value. She needs redemption. It is the story of Beauty and the Beast. We must learn to kiss the Beast in ourselves because God loves us totally and God's love can only change what we are prepared to acknowledge before him.

We have to hold on very hard in order to accept the depths of this search for the inner reality which silence explores in us. Areas of un-love are often hidden by dead, padlocked silences. We don't want to know, and yet we must. These are surely the times when it helps to know someone who will 'hold on' to God for us and with us when the struggle becomes overwhelming. It can overwhelm us at times, but the sea of love flows on if only we will let it. Perhaps at a much later date a little deep-sea diving can salvage unsuspected treasure from what we experienced at the time only as shipwreck.

Perhaps I would be guilty of what the existentialists call 'bad faith' if I left this in such a general form. For various reasons I have been trying to look at the theme of betrayal in my own 'beast'. We find the theme in well-known stories: Eden, Cain and Abel, Jacob and Esau,

Saul, Samson, Job, Peter, Judas and Our Lord. There seems always to be a seed of betrayal in a relationship of trust; we can, after all, only betray and be betrayed by those we love. How easy it is to escape into thoughts of revenge, denial, cynicism or self-betrayal. Yet these experiences can expel us from an untried innocence into consciousness and responsibility. We have to grow up. If there were no betrayal we should never learn of the higher, transcendent forms of love experienced in forgiving and being forgiven. Love and forgiveness are not our possessions, they are gifts. Learning to face the betrayer and the betrayed in me can put me in touch with my need of these gifts, through my sorrow and suffering and my objective turning to God.

Many of us today are perplexed by the problem of violence and, here again, we need to find our own inner variant of the power-driven despot and the martyred victim who surface in bouts of irritation and mean-minded domestic tyranny. Sometimes it is only, as it were, by throwing things at God that we can discover the power of God to re-orientate our drive for power or martyrdom. Peter de Vries' astringent and moving novel *The Blood of the Lamb* is about a man brought up in the strict Calvinist tradition who tries to grow out of it and escape from it. His little daughter begins to die of leukaemia. Eventually he asks God that she might live one more year. The doctor announces that there has been a remission. On the way to the hospital with a cake to celebrate her birthday, the father hears that a chance bug has infected his daughter, and she dies very quickly. In utter dereliction of spirit he goes into a nearby church where he has sometimes reluctantly sheltered, to collect the cake which he had inadvertently left on a seat when he heard the news. On the way out, in a spasm of despair and rage, he throws the cake at the crucifix hanging with outstretched arms above the doorway. Suddenly he sees, through his tears, the patient hands of the crucified Christ move upwards and slowly and gently clear away the spattered mess, and a voice says: 'Suffer little children to come unto me.' And he finds himself, however momentarily, and against all the odds, at the foot of the Cross.[8]

---

[8] Peter De Vries, *The Blood of the Lamb: A Novel* (Chicago University Press, 2005).

The most difficult part of dealing with our Lady Macbeth is that we get things out of proportion and become distinctly humourless. As Kierkegaard said, the mountains within us labour together, and what do they bring forth? A mouse. But at least a timid little mouse is alive and real. I often take, as an image of what I am after, two wooden carvings I have of Don Quixote and Sancho Panza. There is Don Quixote, looking so tall, upright and righteous—asking for trouble—and there is Sancho Panza, relaxed, rounded and at ease on his horse, taking life with a sense of humour.

It is very difficult to talk about these subjects without appearing to be moralising and dreary. What we tend to look for are dramatic experiences, the timeless moments that do, thank God, happen. But all the great religious traditions, including our own, never cease to remind us of the need to 'keep on keeping on' in the nitty-gritty of the ascetical way, the eightfold path, or whatever metaphor each tradition uses. In the Christian tradition the aim has never been to gain self-awareness for its own sake, but through self-awareness to be able to abandon ourselves more completely to an awareness of the God who dwells within us. By virtue of that indwelling, God is deeply participant in our search, but is also that objective Reality towards which all our searchings for inner reality must move.

## Shapes of Silence

We have to recognize that encountering the 'beast' is a lifetime's work, inextricably linked with all our experience of the mystery of good and evil. That heroic man, Alexander Solzhenitsyn, expresses it like this:

> If only it were all so simple! If only there were evil people somewhere insidiously committing evil deeds, and it were necessary only to separate them from the rest of us and destroy them. But the line dividing good and evil cuts through the heart of every human being. And who is willing to destroy a piece of his own heart?
>
> During the life of any heart this line keeps changing place; sometimes it is squeezed one way by exuberant evil and sometimes it shifts

to allow enough space for good to flourish. One and the same human being is, at various ages, under various circumstances, a totally different human being. At times he is close to being a devil, at times to sainthood. But his name doesn't change, and to that name we ascribe the whole lot, good and evil.[9]

If we find that we are still on the journey into silence, in spite of many setbacks, then silence begins to create its own shapes inside us. I want here to look at four shapes of silence beautifully described by Ivan D. Illich in his essay, 'The Eloquence of Silence'.[10] He points out that if we wish to learn a language, it is as important to hear the silences in it as to know the words. He likens language to a cord of silence, with words as the knots. The silence and the sounds together produce the particular rhythm of the language.

*The silence of availability.* This is the experience of necessary passivity, availability. The word is conceived and rooted in silence. We need to expose ourselves to the creative Spirit: 'Be it unto me'; 'Here am I'.

*The silence of growth.* This is the silence of gestation, the internal growth and nurture of the word after conception. We have to close in to prepare the word for its eventual birth at the proper moment. This is the silence before and between words: prayer in which words have the courage to swim in a sea of silence.

*Silence beyond words.* This is pure silence, after words have done all they can, the silence of lovers. This is the origin and completion of all words when 'we must aim at that Silence which alone God is in himself'.

*The silence of the Pietà.* This is the silence of suffering and the mystery of death. This is not the passive acceptance of the Word of God —

---

[9] Alexander Solzhenitsyn, *The Gulag Archipelago 1918–1956: An Experiment in Literary Investigation I–II*, trans. Thomas P. Whitney (Book Club Associates, 1974), 168.

[10] The essay is in Ivan D. Illich, *Celebration of Awareness: A Call for Institutional Revolution*, Penguin Education Special (Penguin Books, 1973).

*Fiat;* nor the manly acceptance of Gethsemane—obedience; it is the mysterious silence in which God can descend into hell, the silence of freely-willed powerlessness, the self-emptying of God, the fulfilment of the mystery of the Incarnation.

All these and other shapes of silence we may find coming to us in image, symbol, story, icon—gradually making their own room inside us if only we let them. Small is beautiful. Sometimes we have to spend a long time nursing one small truth until we receive another. 'it is required of stewards that they be found trustworthy' (1 Cor. 4:2).

## Enduring Silence

I think the inner discipline of the practice of silent prayer can help us to endure in the face of much doubt and disturbance of our faith. If absolute faith were always possible it would hardly be faith. Carrying our own share of honest doubt is surely part of the journey into a living faith. The process of carrying our faith and our doubt seems to me to need a good deal of honest silence and endurance, as well as the search for meaning in words. In Isaiah, silence and hope appear to be specially linked. Where there is silence there is a nesting place for hope—pure hope; not hope of anything in particular—just *hope.*

Also, and this is the other side of the coin, there is no doubt that silence needs to be endured with an incredible amount of patience and quiet persistence. The image of a journey that we so often use in speaking of the spiritual life can be misleading if it predisposes us to think that we should always be on the move, that something should be 'happening'. The forty years in the wilderness can hardly have seemed a journey; a grim endurance test, more likely, with everyone needing all their strength just to plod on, so as not to slide down a spiral of hopelessness and despair. There are times in prayer when the desert seems gritty, refreshing water is short, Brother Camel—the body—has 'got the hump', and there is little to be done but pull the blanket over our heads and sit it out, and not go sloping off after some tempting mirage.

## Living with Silence

Often when we turn from our own subjective experiencing towards God we find ourselves saying, 'Truly you are a God who hides himself.' (Is. 45:15) God appears to be silent, so silent as to frighten us into thinking that God has gone.

We must first try to discover to what extent we are being like Oedipus—who plucked out his eyes and then cried against the dark. Using a similar image Catherine of Genoa said: 'If a person would see properly in spiritual matters, let them pluck out the eyes of their own presumption.' But without the eyes of presumption we often feel blind indeed. I sometimes find that seeking silence and self-awareness can lead into a dark inner apathy, a sort of vacuum which sucks into itself all one's most dire egotism. Then we can become absorbed in the illusions and idolatries woven by our self-reflecting narcissism.

On the other hand, the dark unknownness of God and the silence of God are very much a mysterious part of Christian experience for which it is difficult to find adequate words. I know that I have been helped in struggling with this not only by the apophatic[11] tradition of Eastern Orthodoxy but also by Martin Buber, the great Jewish philosopher. He was sure that people in the present age have confined God too much to their own subjectivity, losing God in the convolutions of their own psyches. We have abandoned the life of faith and sold ourselves out to forms of what he called 'psychological gnosticism', to an 'I know' attitude, where we are more concerned with power and knowledge than with love and trust. He was also sure that we have become too impersonal about what lies outside ourselves. The result is that we lack spontaneity and cannot step into relationship with the Living God. We must, Buber said, begin to penetrate existence by active love; then we would find the signs of God were there: they are spoken into life, not above it.

---

[11] From *apophasis*—negation, denial. Apophatic theology is that kind which denies all attributes to God such as goodness, wisdom, majesty, simplicity, in order, as Gregory Palamas says, 'to draw near to the Unknown in the darkness of absolute unknowing'.

In an essay called 'At the Turning', Martin Buber talks of the age-old Jewish cry, 'Will He allow injustice to reign further'?

> How is life with God still possible in a time in which there is an Auschwitz? ... The estrangement has become too cruel, the hiddenness too deep ... dare we urge the survivors, 'Call to him for he is kind; his mercy endures forever'?[12]

Of Job he writes:

> And he receives an answer from God. But what God says to him does not answer the charge, it does not even touch upon it. The true answer Job receives is God's appearance only, only this, that distance turns into nearness, that his eyes 'see him'. Nothing is explained; nothing adjusted; wrong has not become right; nor cruelty, kindness. Nothing has happened but that man again hears God's address.
>
> How is it with us? do we stand overcome before the hidden face of God? ... No, rather even now we contend, we too, with God ... though his coming appearance resemble no earlier one, we shall recognise again our cruel and merciful Lord.

## Presence in Silence

So then, if we can do without the explanations and the adjustments, we are able to experience prayer as an unending pursuit of the Presence. Then silence is the place of the Presence, and at its heart is God.

God's presence cannot be conjured or constrained, but if we wait upon him—a waiting that might mean asking, seeking, knocking, or *just waiting*—in faith, hope and love, we shall see what is given us to see. Buber points out that Moses did not see God's face, but he learnt his ways. Our Lord's face may be obscure, but we know his ways—of love and justice and self-emptying—and we see him in our neighbours, who need our caring and our prayers.

---

[12] Martin Buber, 'At the Turning', in *At the Turning: Three Addresses on Judaism* (New York: Farrar, Strauss & Young, 1952).

How can we speak of that mysterious Presence at the heart of silence? Perhaps only through the cherishing of his Name and its mysteries. The real Hebrew meaning, we are told, of the mystery of the Name, rendered in our biblical versions as 'I am that I am', should be, 'I shall be there as I shall be there'. God's presence is assured; the form it will take is not. If we wish to recognize the form of the Living God in each moment, then we must keep close and be watchful with the love of all our heart, mind and strength. The great forms or images of God were born of encounter, and they change: You are this… and yet not this…

That great and humble man, George Appleton, at one time Archbishop in Jerusalem, expressed this way of approach in one of his prayers:

> O Christ, my Lord, again and again
> I have said with Mary Magdalene,
> 'They have taken away my Lord
> and I know not where they have laid him.'
> I have been desolate and alone.
> And thou hast found me again, and I know
> that what has died is not thou, my Lord,
> but only my idea of thee,
> the image which I have made to preserve
> what I have found, and to be my security.
> I shall make another image, O Lord,
> better than the last.
> That too must go, and all successive images,
> until I come to the blessed vision of thyself,
> O Christ my Lord.[13]

The movement into deeper silence will always bring us into touch with the mysteries of life and human experience: suffering, death, love, evil. We need to bear in mind a distinction, drawn by Gabriel Marcel in his book, *Being and Having*, between those problems one can face and

---

[13] *The Oxford Book of Prayer*, ed. George Appleton (Oxford: Oxford University Press, 1985), 147, no. 498.

work on, recognizing them as ultimately soluble, and those problems which are mysteries, yielding their meaning only according to the quality of being we are able to bring to them.

There come times when inner silence is experienced as an utter void. God is not only the firm ground and substance of my being, but also the abyss. The silence is no longer me-shaped, but infinitely God-shaped. It is a terrible thing to fall into the hands of the Living God (even if, as has been said, it is a worse thing to fall out of them). The abyss takes us in an absolutely real way into the meaning of the phrase, 'the fear of the Lord'. Like St Patrick and his Trinitarian breastplate, we need something to which to bind ourselves—the Prayer of the Name: 'Lord Jesus Christ, Son of the living God, have mercy on me, a sinner'; 'My God and my all'; or some other rhythmical prayer, can be a boat in which to embark on the deeper seas of silence. We can entrust ourselves to it; we can lash ourselves to it when the seas are rough, or rest in it when becalmed.

The tradition and teaching associated with the Jesus Prayer in the Orthodox Church is very rich. To put it briefly, from where I stand I call upon the Name of the Lord (neither, it is said, can I call him Lord unless the Spirit calls through me), *Lord Jesus Christ ... have mercy on me* in all the mysteries of my created being; *have mercy on me, a sinner.* At ever new depths I turn in wonder and dependence on the mysteries of the Trinity and the Incarnation. And from the depths of the abyss into which that plunges me, again I turn and call *Lord ...* to immerse myself once more in the Source of the mysteries of the faith.

There is a phrase, *nexus mysteriorum,* once much used, I believe, which is an attempt to express the internal consistency and inter-relatedness of the ultimate mysteries of the world. The Jesus Prayer is certainly one of the ways in which we can experience this nexus. The movement of the prayer is infinite because it increasingly puts in the heart of our being the silent heart of all being, the divine Name. And the whole offering in the prayer is the same movement that we experience in the Eucharist and in all sacramental living, and is never, in the Christian tradition, separated from them.

Martin Buber met many people who experienced difficulty in using the word 'God'. I want to quote a passage where he responds to this difficulty:

'Yes,' I said, 'it is the most heavily-laden of all human words. None has become so soiled, so mutilated. Just for this reason I may not abandon it. Generations of men have laid the burden of their anxious lives upon this word and weighed it to the ground; it lies in the dust and bears their whole burden. The races of man with their religious factions have torn the word to pieces; they have killed for it and died for it, and it bears their finger-marks and their blood. Where might I find a word like it to describe the highest! If I took the purest, most sparkling concept from the inner treasure-chamber of the philosophers, I could only capture thereby an unbinding product of thought. I could not capture the presence of Him whom the generations of men have honoured and degraded with their awesome living and dying. I do indeed mean Him whom the hell-tormented and heaven-storming generations of men mean. Certainly they draw caricatures and write 'God' underneath; they murder one another and say, 'In God's name'. But when all madness and delusion fall to dust, when they stand over against Him in the loneliest darkness and no longer say 'He, He' but rather sigh 'Thou', shout 'Thou', all of them the one word, and when they then add 'God', is it not the real God whom they all implore, the One Living God, the God of the children of man? Is it not He who *hears* them? And just for this reason is not the word 'God', the word of appeal, the word which has become a *name*, consecrated in all human tongues for all times? We must esteem those who interdict it because they rebel against the injustice and wrong which are so readily referred to 'God' for authorisation. But we must not give it up. How understandable it is that some suggest we should remain silent about the 'last things' for a time in order that the misused words may be redeemed! But they are not to be redeemed *thus*. We cannot cleanse the word 'God' and we cannot make it whole; but, defiled and mutilated as it is, we can raise it from the ground and set it over an hour of great care.'[14]

---

[14] Martin Buber, *Eclipse of God: Studies in the Relation between Religion and Philosophy* (London: Victor Gollancz, 1953), 17–18, I. 'Prelude: Report on Two Talks'.

The Presence, within us and yet totally beyond us, is not an alien intrusive force but can become perceptible to us as a living Person with whom we enter into dialogue — what Buber called 'dialogically perceivable'. How much we can learn from the Old Testament patriarchs as they argue with God; and from the Psalms when the speaker changes his attitude through being prepared to enter into honest dialogue and say what is going on inside! I think we have to relearn what is meant by asking. It is not bullying or cajoling, nor is it falling over backwards to say, 'far be it from me…, but…' It is learning the simplicity of a dependence that *can* ask.

## Shared Silence

Although the journey into God is one that we must each undertake individually, in ever-increasing depth, yet we know that we are also called together; we need each other, we are inescapably part of each other. My want is part of the want of the whole. My peace, joy, search, need, are part of the whole. One of Buber's main insights is that of 'the between'. God, the eternal Thou, is not the possession of any of us, but is experienced 'between us' in any genuine meeting.

Yet how do we find a meaningful outward expression of this *koinonia*, fellowship, when so many of the organized structures fail to satisfy deeply-felt needs? Some of us have found that to explore silence in prayer in small groups is a help. I realized what an upholding and strengthening experience this could be when I shared in the prayer hours of a contemplative community and felt it was a pity this sort of sharing was not more widely attempted outside such communities. I had also been a Friend (Quaker) and had learnt that it was possible to maintain a disciplined and meaningful form of meeting in which silence was the binding factor. I believe that in the discipline and depth of silence we can begin to come into a quite new, living relationship with the silent, unknown shapes of God, the God who speaks through silences. I think this actual sharing can also take us into a new awareness of being part of the Communion of Saints. Fr Gilbert Shaw, again in his *Pilgrim's Book of Prayers*, says:

It is natural to our loneliness and fitting to our humility to ask the prayers and care of our friends. It would be indeed unneighbourly if we restricted this operation to the limited circle of those whom we could know in the flesh, and ignored the number of those whom we might come to know by faith.[15]

Philosophers like Michael Polanyi have sought to show that much of our knowledge is based on what he calls, in his book of that name, 'the tacit dimension'. In both Christian and Jewish traditions there are moving descriptions of encounters between people in which shared communication through silence meant more than words could ever express. There is the famous meeting between St Louis, King of France, and Brother Egidio, the Franciscan. They had longed to meet; when they did they embraced, remained long in silence, and parted. Brother Egidio was asked why they did not speak and replied:

from the minute we embraced, the light of divine wisdom showed his heart to me and mine to him. By the workings of God we looked into each other, knowing what I wanted to say to him and what he wanted to say to me better and with greater comfort than if we had spoken. Because of the inadequacy of all words, which cannot clearly express the secret mysteries of God, there would have been disappointment rather than comfort.[16]

And then there is the delightful Hasidic tale of Rabbi Mendel of Vorki. Rabbi Mendel and his Hasidim once sat at table in silence. The silence was so deep that a fly on the wall could be heard. After the meal a visiting Rabbi said to his neighbour, 'What a table we had today. I was probed so deeply that I thought my veins would burst, but I managed to hold my own and answer every question I was asked!' Rabbi Mendel lived in a period of Hasidic decline when people felt immersed in a dark and corrupt time. For him silence was the way, a living and effective force.

---

[15] Shaw, *A Pilgrim's Book of Prayers*, xx.
[16] In Brother Ugolino, *The Little Flowers: The Life of St Francis*, Baronius Press Classics (Virginia Beach: Baronius Press Ltd, 2006), Part I, ch. XXIV.

Some of the animal ethologists make very interesting assessments that we might do well to meditate upon. Robert Ardrey, in his book *The Social Contract*, writes this:

> The just society, as I see it, is one in which sufficient order protects members, whatever their diverse endowments, and sufficient disorder provides every individual with opportunities to develop his genetic endowment, whatever that may be.[17]

He also points out that diversity is the material of evolution and that the pursuit of security (and conformity) is only reward-bearing if you do not have it.

Those of us who do meet in groups, with the sharing of silent prayer at the heart of them, need to be aware of fruitful tensions between protection and development, diversity and risk, if we do not want to become institutionalized in the wrong sense. Thomas Merton says somewhere that to become a personality you have to be exclusive; in order to become a mature human being you have to be inclusive. Something of the same nature surely applies to our group experiences.

Yet at the same time, while being flexible, we have to be disciplined about what goes on. Are we there for a therapeutic purpose or not? If we are going into the field of trying to cope with psychological problems directly, then we must know a great deal about group dynamics and recognize that some people only feel real when they are the centre of attention. But it seems to me that if we can curb our natural curiosity and our desire to be involved and to help, a simple acknowledgement of need, and a lifting of it to God, provides a middle way by which we can best help each other. There is an obvious danger that if we are not disciplined then the strongest or the sickest psyche may dominate the atmosphere of the group, leading to great difficulties and psychic contamination, and the true interior development of the many may be cramped or crippled. I doubt whether a silent prayer group is the right place for very sick souls and perhaps we

---

[17] Robert Ardrey, *The Social Contract: A Personal Inquiry into the Evolutionary Sources of Order and Disorder* (New York: Dell Publishing, 1974), 3.

should be rigorous about this early enough and not allow the situation to get out of hand. There are other occasions for the active expression of love and concern.

There is an idea around that members of a group should be experiencing a 'high' most of the time. This, of course, is nonsense. Life is not all 'highs', and plateaux are as important as peaks. I think that it can sometimes help to put into words, simply, in conversation afterwards, the 'feeling' of the silence: 'Sticky tonight', or 'helpful tonight'. This can enable the less experienced members to go away without a sense of guilt and 'It's all me' about it. Of course there are bad patches, and we must watch the quality of what we are sharing. There is the story of the old countryman who, faced with a Quaker meeting, said, 'What's the good of going to hear them as has nowt to say?' That can be balanced against another remark: 'If they'd said anything I could have answered them.'

I would like to recall two Quaker accounts of the positive value of corporate silence. Friends, after all, have been sharing silence for a long time. The first is that of Caroline E. Stephen in 1908:

> In the united stillness of a truly 'gathered' meeting there is a power known only by experience, and mysterious even when most familiar.[18]

The second account is from the Scottish Quaker convert of the seventeenth century, Robert Barclay:

> Not by strength of arguments or by a particular disquisition of each doctrine, and convincement of my understanding thereby, came [I] to receive and bear witness of the Truth, but by being secretly reached by [the] Life. For, when I came into the silent assemblies of God's people, I felt a secret power among them, which touched my heart; and as I gave way unto it I found the evil weakening in me and the good raised up; and so I became thus knit and united unto them, hungering more and more after the increase of this power and life whereby I might feel myself perfectly redeemed; and indeed this is

---

[18] Caroline E. Stephen, *Light Arising: Thoughts on the Central Radiance* (1908), 68–9.

the surest way to become a Christian; to whom afterwards the knowledge and understanding of principles will not be wanting.[19]

There can be in a shared silence something that strengthens, upholds, teaches us, once we realize that it is not just a case of tolerating each other's waywardness but a turning in love together to that which unites us — the presence of God.

## Conclusion

I will end by quoting a rhythmic prayer, 'Seeking Wholeness', which Mother Mary Clare SLG adapted from a section of *The Face of Love* by Fr Gilbert Shaw:[20]

> *Most loving Lord, hold me fast to live by you*
> *in all occasions of my life,*
> *in the busyness of daily life and in my sleeping hours.*
>
> *Keep my heart united to yourself*
> *to be the temple of the Holy Spirit*
> *that he revealing you to me*
> *may energise my soul*
> *to be more fully one with you.*
>
> *If I forget you in the manifold confusions*
> *of all the outward passing things,*
> *still the inmost depths of memory and will*
> *that all my thinking may return*
> *to know that you indwell my heart.*

---

[19] Robert Barclay (1648–90), quoted in *Quaker Faith and Practice: The Book of Christian Discipline of the Yearly Meeting of the Religious Society of Friends (Quakers) in Britain* (Quaker Peace & Service, 4th edn, 2009), 19: 21.

[20] Gilbert Shaw, *The Face of Love: Meditations on the Way of the Cross* (SLG Press, 1977).

*Cleanse the complex patterns of my unconsciousness*
  *that nothing may distort my will*
  *or turn my heart from loving you,*
  *from serving you in spirit and in truth.*

*May every thought and action of the day*
  *be unified and offered to your praise;*
  *and while I sleep may my heart wake,*
    *giving unto you my love*
    *to glorify your name,*
  *that all that is not wholly reconciled to you*
  *may be resolved and simplified by love,*
  *the love which is the knowledge of yourself.*

*Look well, O soul, upon yourself*
  *lest spiritual ambition*
  *should mislead and blind you*
  *to your essential task—*
    *to wait in quietness:*
    *to knock and persevere in humble faith.*

*Knock; knock in love,*
  *nor fail to keep your place before the door*
  *that when Christ wills—and not before—*
  *he may open unto you the treasures of his love.*

*Grant me therefore humility of soul*
  *that I may grow in penitence*
  *dependent on the Holy Spirit's light.*

# BIBLIOGRAPHICAL NOTES

All Rabbinic and Hasidic tales in this paper are in Martin Buber, *Tales of the Hasidim*, two vols.: *The Early Masters* (Schocken Books, 1947) and *Later Masters* (Schocken Books, 1948).

Teaching on the Jewish understanding of the Divine Name is contained in Martin Buber's books *I and Thou*, trans. Walter Kaufmann (T. & T. Clark Ltd., 1971), and *The Prophetic Faith* (Harper Torchbooks, 1960). See also 'Buber's understanding of the Divine Name related to Bible, Targum and Midrash' by Pamela Vermes in the *Journal of Jewish Studies*, 24/2 (Autumn 1973), 147–166.

A classic exposition of the Jesus Prayer in Orthodox spirituality is to be found in Kallistos Ware's *The Power of the Name* (SLG Press, 1974). There is a very useful introduction by the same author in Igumen Chariton of Valamo, *The Art of Prayer: An Orthodox Anthology*, trans. E. Kadloubovsky and G. E. H. Palmer (Faber & Faber, 1971). Another helpful short work is by A Monk of the Eastern Church [Fr Lev Gillet], *On the Invocation of the Name of Jesus* (Fellowship of St Alban and St Sergius, 1960).

George Appleton's book, *One Man's Prayers* (SPCK 1977), contains many prayers which express a profound ability to grapple with the secular insights of our day, for instance in the field of psychology, combined with a deep living faith in the objective reality of God and the need for our personal commitment and response to God.

Gilbert Shaw's books, *A Pilgrim's Book of Prayers* and *The Face of Love*, both originally published by A. R. Mowbray, are published by SLG Press. For current availability, and for e-book editions, see www.slgpress.co.uk

# Mary, the Flower and Fruit of Worship: The Mother of God in the Orthodox Tradition

## Approaching Mary

We can only approach the Mother of God with more silence than words. The words we find are only what can be held in cupped hands, out of the great sea of meanings which flows all around her. She is, in the West as well as in the East, the star of that sea, the guide for lost and weary travellers. For many women in our age, for a variety of cogent and sometimes tragic reasons, her star has not been visible through the lowering clouds of controversy, anger and painful searching about the place and meaning of women and men together in the Church. Some of us who have entered the Orthodox Church in adult life have come to experience her presence slowly, yet surely. Some of us have been helped by Bishop Kalllistos's devotion to the Mother of God expressed in celebration of the mysteries, when she is so constantly evoked, or in talks on pilgrimages to Walsingham or to the Ecumenical Society of the Blessed Virgin Mary.

I remember Nicolas and Militza Zernov talking to me of the importance of the Mother of God in worship and iconography. 'As goes Mary, so goes the church', they would say. The future of the Church is intimately linked with the living life and prayer of the Mother of God in our midst. She is in our midst in worship, always pointing beyond herself to Christ. How important is that gesture of transcendence, which Christ, too, makes in his earthly life to the Father, and to the coming of the Spirit; which the Father makes to the beloved Son; which the Spirit makes in our hearts as we pray: the beyond that is yet in the midst. The Mother of God is in the midst with open heart, revealing in the icon of Tenderness (so commonly found now in the West, too) a tender love being met by a tender love, or her presence in the heart of suffering at the foot of the Cross, or in the heart waiting on God at Pentecost in the upper room. In such wise the Mother of God leads us to the place of the heart, the deep centre of our theandric personhood. As she, like her Son, 'ever lives to make intercession for us' in that 'place of the heart', herself a living symbol of hesychia, or inner stillness, in what other place would we choose to stand if we were living our life at its deepest and fullest?

In one of his poems the western Catholic poet Gerard Manley Hopkins compares the Mother of God to the air we breathe.[1] The Mother of God is the air we breathe in worship, the atmosphere of the church at its deepest and fullest. In Orthodox worship there are particular moments when a palpable attention and devotion are noticeable among the worshippers. One such moment is always in the making of the sign of the Cross and the looks directed to the icon of the Mother of God when she is addressed in the litanies. 'Commemorating our all-holy, pure, most blessed and glorious Lady, Mother of God and ever-virgin Mary with all the saints, let us entrust ourselves and one another and our whole life to Christ our God'—even as she entrusted herself. In the Orthodox tradition it is often said that Mary, Theotokos, does not belong to the outer world of declared dogma but to the secret inner life of the Church, to be discovered there. She is present as the flower and fruit of worship, ripened in tradition.

So where dogma is experienced in its seeds, in its roots, in worship and in prayer, Mary, as flower and fruit, is revealed. The stories we hear about her in worship surround and protect the truth of the incarnation of the Son, the second Person of the Trinity. Many of the stories come out of the *Protevangelium of James*. In historical terms we cannot set out to prove events from them. But they are 'telling tales', effective and affective, revelatory stories rooted in faith and belief. As we repeat them year by year in the great cycle of feasts and fasts, they become a creative matrix of story and image, of mystery and silence, that nourish and 'hold' the truths of faith which maintain us.

The deepest level of the human soul is where *poesis* happens—a creative energy which throws up for us dreams and images and is symbol-making and story-telling. 'The symbol touches the depth long before it reaches the surface';[2] long before it engenders thought and rationality. What from the point of view of rationality we call rhetoric, or

---

[1] *Poems of Gerard Manley Hopkins* (Oxford: Oxford University Press, 1950 [1930]), 99.

[2] Gaston Bachelard, *The Poetics of Space* (Boston: Beaca, 1940), 131.

figures of speech, refers to the deepest activities of the human soul when we learn to read it, to know its transformations and to use it creatively, 'under the Protection'. That deep place of making gives rise to thought but it is wise for thought to keep its tap root in the creative matrix, where truths are invocatory, celebratory, proclamatory, rather than set out as rational propositions. That is why when inquirers want Orthodox people to say something about ourselves we have to say: 'Come and worship with us.' You can't just learn the truth in talk or discussion or reading. You have to meet it in worship, in the making, in touch with the creative matrix. In that meeting and making of worship you will find us always commemorating the one who is 'more honourable than the cherubim and incomparably more glorious than the seraphim, our all-holy, pure, most blessed and glorious Mother of God and ever-virgin Mary...' There is always a certain silence around the mysteries, an awe in the worshipping experience of God's love and truth and presence. And so it is for the Mother of God, too. There is a certain silence around her mysteries. Yet this numinous, awe-inspiring and luminous, light-giving silence has always been endlessly inspirational. One moment we have teaching on the apophatic need to move beyond images, to honour silence and venerate the mysteries, the next moment we have images pouring forth as if from a breathtaking treasure-house. There is even a risk of satiety for those of us not born and bred in this tradition. The Akathist hymn to the Mother of God (used particularly on Fridays in Lent) with its flow of images drawn from cosmos and biblical culture, weaves a glorious robe of attributions around the Mother of God, 'Unwedded Bride; Bride without bridegroom':

> Hail, beam of the spiritual Sun;
> Hail, ray of the moon that never wanes;
> Hail, lightning flash that shines upon our souls;
> Hail, thunder... Hail, dawn... Hail, spring... water... cup...
> Hail, Height hard to climb even for thoughts of men,
> Hail, Depth hard to scan, even for the eyes of angels.
> Hail, Bride without bridegroom.[3]

---

[3] *Akathistos Hymn to the Most Holy Mother of God,* trans. Kallistos Ware (Ecumenical Society of the Blessed Virgin Mary, 1987), Ikos One, 18.

Again, the Lamentations in the services of Holy Week are expressive and full of deep emotion, almost causing through their reiterative rhythms a physical withdrawal into reticence, endurance and silence around the mystery of the Passion:

> When she beheld her Son and Lord hanging on the cross, the pure Virgin was torn by grief and weeping bitterly with the other women, and she cried out: 'Woe is me! I see thee, dearest and beloved Child, hanging on the cross and my heart is wounded bitterly... How am I deprived of Him who is my hope, my gladness, of my Son and God. Woe is me, my heart is filled with anguish...'[4]

Indeed, rhythm and repetition in liturgical forms seem to carry a deep experience of feminine discourse that we otherwise meet in the rituals, rhythms and repetitions around the birth and nurture of small babies and children, as well as in expressions of grief and mourning around death. Learning to live in this creative matrix we discover slowly over time what it means to be Orthodox—to find the rhythms of its tides and waves, how it ebbs and flows around us, carrying us. We don't need to sustain it except by our cooperation in it, but it sustains us.

In that matrix in worship we meet the Mother of God as the pivotal point through which we turn, bringing the cosmos with us, through our personhood, towards God, offering ourselves through her. As we say at Christmas:

> What shall we offer thee, O Christ, who for our sakes has appeared on earth as man? Every creature made by thee offers thee thanks. The angels offer thee a hymn; the heavens, a star; the Magi, gifts; the shepherds, their wonder; the earth, a cave; the wilderness, a manger; and we offer thee a Virgin Mother.[5]

---

[4] Holy Friday, Small Compline, canticle one, from *The Lenten Triodion*, trans. Mother Maria and Archimandrite Kallistos Ware (London: Faber & Faber, 1978), 617.

[5] Vespers of the Nativity of Christ, from *The Festal Menaion*, trans. Mother Mary and Archimandrite Kallistos Ware (London: Faber & Faber, 1984), 254.

She is our great offering through whom we offer ourselves to God. At times we have to struggle with the pains, fears, doubts and glories of our individual journey and struggle to follow St Paul's injunction:

> I appeal to you therefore, brothers and sisters, by the mercies of God, to present your bodies as a living sacrifice, holy and acceptable to God, which is your spiritual worship. (Rom. 12:1)

But in our shared worship we can offer ourselves in and through and with the Mother of God; an act of simple joy even in the midst of suffering, in gratitude for the incarnation. At those moments we are deeply aware of the one who is called most truly the 'Joy of all Creation'.

## Ritual

It is always impossible to present an even remotely adequate account of the experience of the rite, which is only discovered through participation in it, sharing in the mysterious, corporate, sacramental and symbolic 'language' of ritual which is not reducible to the language of the conscious individual self.[6] We can only say, 'Come and see.'

What I do know is that it has been a transformative experience for me as woman, as psychotherapist and as a human person, caught up in the theandric vision of what it means to be truly human: 'your life is hidden with Christ in God', as St Paul says (Col. 3:3). Yet I remain terribly conscious of the struggles both within myself and within those who share their lives with me. Many people have been alienated from the Mother of God because of what the history of religious culture has made of Mary in terms of the history of women. The Mother of God is a tender, protective presence and companion to the suffering, the poor and the afflicted. I do not think she minds if we bring her our problems and our searchings about who she is and what she means for us. Some of the struggles may seem alien to those born into the Orthodox tradition and who have always 'known' the presence of the Mother of God.

---

[6] Roger Grainger, *The Language of the Rite* (London: Darton, Longman and Todd, 1975), 7ff.

Some of the conflicts as people express them can seem distasteful, so that any discussion of 'woman' in some Orthodox circles will be dismissed as secularized feminism. Mercifully, there are people like Bishop Kallistos and Elisabeth Behr-Sigel who encourage us to remain open to the pressing questions about our understanding of sexuality and gender within the understanding of the Church, priesthood and other related and sometimes burning issues.

Marina Warner, in her fascinating book about the Marian tradition in the West, *Alone of All Her Sex*, points even in the title to something of what the problems for women have been about. The title is taken from a translation of Caelius Sedulius:

> She... had no peer
> Either in our first mother or in all women
> Who were to come. But alone of all her sex She pleased the Lord.[7]

'Alone of all her sex...' encapsulates the danger, as women see it, that sometimes the Mother of God is celebrated as so special, so different, that we lose a sense of her solidarity with us and that is an appalling loss. She ceases to be that representative 'Everywoman' who is also 'Everyman', through whom we offer ourselves to Christ as she did. The application of Mariology has led, tragically, to certain kinds of encultured trouble. It has seemed at times to promote a particular image of woman which has certain beauties and may provide an idealized image of how men would sometimes like women to be, but assuredly does not carry the total reality of women's lives and their way to God. For what it has sometimes done in family life or in schools (particularly some convent schools) is to bring about a rather narrow band of piety, of what was acceptable behaviour for *a* woman. It was conveyed that she should be quiet, preferably silent, humble, pure and good, in a domestic interior, devoted and submissive, knowing her place. Girls brought up in that strict tradition will sometimes talk about how much they gained from it (plenty of convent-raised girls have been spirited lasses!) but also about the difficulties that were

---

[7] Marina Warner, *Alone of All Her Sex: The Myth and the Cult of the Virgin Mary* (Picador, 1990).

engendered in it. They feel that they learned an ambiguity about the body (their embodied reality as women) with a sense of shame that took a lot of overcoming. They felt bad and ignorant about their sexuality. They could not talk about menstruation without much shame. They found it was difficult, even if they had 'saved themselves' for marriage, to cope with desire and sexuality within marriage. They felt they were acceptable if they were kind and nice and clean and good. But alas! They also sometimes found that they wanted to be clever, well-educated, to take part in the public world, to argue for the sake of truth, to be angry in the cause of justice, to be stroppy and sexy and searching; in fact women who did not know their place in terms of traditional piety. So the problems leave us in the midst of things, always in the womb of things, always on the road, travelling and searching women—and we have to be able to bring all that reality to the Mother of God.

There is an extreme danger that across the centuries the Mother of God has been presented as less human in some ways than her Son, somehow not being tempted, more remote from our fallen humanity, and less a woman of desire who has to find the long road to compassionate and mutual selfless love. Theologically, that represents a supreme irony. She who became known as 'Theotokos' in order to protect the truth of incarnation can become in religious culture dangerously dehumanized, discarnate. That is one temptation, but there is another. If we place in Mary certain characteristics of compassion, mercy, of nearness, of tenderness and leave other things to Christ, such as stern judge, Pantocrator—it leads to a devastating split in how we experience the divine. There are a number of amusing stories which illustrate this dangerous tendency. For instance, Christ came to St Peter at the gates one day and said: 'How is it that there are so many people around in heaven? I can't believe they were all meant to be here.' St Peter answers, 'Well, I do my best. I say no, but the Mother of God is round at the back door letting them in.' It is a story that touches matters that are recognizable and arguable between men and women, and how characteristics on the human plane can get unhelpfully split between the sexes too. It also touches the nervy place in all of us about the Last Judgement.

Discussions about sexuality and gender have often tended to be acrimonious. At times women have expressed much anger towards men and their apparent hold on power and domination: sometimes more apparent than real. It helped me recently, when I was looking through a book of paintings of Mary in all their richness and variety, to realize that they were all of them painted by men. I realized again that there is something about this image of woman, Virgin and Mother, that speaks particularly to a reality in man's soul. Perhaps the image expresses the tender, virginal side of man, and the longing for the mother, which as women we do well to treasure and cherish and respect, even if at times we are having to talk with them firmly about our earthy and varied humanity as women. I experience the insistent hand of the Spirit on our current preoccupations, as if God is wanting to restore a fuller Christian anthropology—and is having to find a new way to reach us as encultured images and ideas have become too ingrained and stereotyped. No transformative change happens without unrest, conflict and risk, but sometimes the living God requires it of us.

## Images

So, then, if we turn to the great images of the Mother of God as Virgin Mother, how can we learn to understand them? To quote a simple and telling poem by San Juan de la Cruz, in translation:

> The Virgin comes walking
> The Word in her womb:
> Could you not give her
> Place in your room?[8]

What is the meaning of the Virgin? We can ask questions that end in reductive biology and a dismissal of the whole story. But if we ask instead a 'Who?' question, it can lead us to the hypothesis of the person. She who is Virgin: what does that mean for us? We know that biblical and patristic

---

[8] From *Centred on Love: The Poems of Saint John of the Cross*, trans. Marjorie Flower OC (New South Wales: Varroville Carmel, 1983).

stories of Mary's virginity safeguard the incarnation. 'Virgin' carries with it a spiritual meaning, which is that of a total givenness to God. 'She learnt what she was FOR', as a student once said. We speak of her three-fold virginity—the one who was given to God, in innocence, in experience and ever. The 'ever-ness' informs all the rest: a total givenness to God. Here we sense that virginity is not a state, and is certainly not a possession, but is rather an eschatological reality. It is a reality that calls to us from the fulness of time, from the pleroma, from the way things will be because that is how they truly are ontologically. This reality is not just a perfectionist ideal, which floats above us and haunts us and taunts us for not being able to measure up to it, but a reality, a deep truth in which we have to learn to participate. It has its place in origins, in innocence, in the beginning—in body and biology. It moves through experience, through fallenness and our struggles to find our true personhood and transformation in Christ. It exercises an eschatological pull on our lives, full of future promise. How can we make real that total givenness to God? Virginity in that sense is something into which we must grow. It lies ahead of us in our becoming ever more real in givenness. It is linked with our restoration in Christ, our transformation in the Spirit, our divinization. It makes of our lives a theandric reality. It comes through our working together with the energies of God. It is an ascetic path which can include all our brokenness, all the consequences of the Fall. We can discover again and again that the touch of God restores virginity, our capacity for total givenness to God—when we come in tears, in sorrow, with a desire for *metanoia*. Thomas Merton describes that kind of virginity:

> At the centre of our being is a point of nothingness ('le point vierge') which is untouched by sin and by illusion, a point of pure truth, a point which belongs entirely to God, which is never at our disposal, from which God disposes of our lives, which is inaccessible to the fantasies of our own minds or the brutalities of our own will. This little point of nothingness in us and of absolute poverty is the pure glory of God in us. It is his Name written in us.[9]

---

[9] Thomas Merton, *Conjectures of a Guilty Bystander* (Burns and Oates, 1965), 142.

Sometimes I find the approach to that reality can come through the phrase 'spiritual integrity'. I can use that phrase with people who are sexually active or celibate, and particularly with those who suffer, believers or not. Our fallen state can lead to the most appalling abuse — spiritual, emotional, sexual — of other human beings. There are always the *anawim* (the poor of the biblical tradition) whose integrity of body, soul and spirit has been invaded overwhelmingly, who have been battered by the accidents of birth or nurture and who feel totally broken, abject (i.e. thrown away) and lacking in any sense of their own integrity. It sometimes takes a long and loving journey with a compassionate other before they can find a sense of that 'virgin point' within, expressed in Psalm 139:

> For it was you who formed my inward parts; you knit me together in my mother's womb. ... My frame was not hidden from you, when I was being made in secret, intricately woven in the depths of the earth. Your eyes beheld my unformed substance. (Ps. 139:13, 15, 16)

There is an integrity, a virginity, which can be restored in Christ, through encounter, through baptism, through sacraments, through feasts and fasts, through supreme spiritual effort, *podvig*, through tears, through failure, through love — through God's grace enabling all our efforts, forgiving all our abject failures. Virginity in that sense represents a potent integrity. And so we offer ourselves through the one who stands in our midst as Virgin — and with her and through her prayers we find that we too are capable of God. With her we can offer God our finite freedom and entrust it to his eternal freedom, in order that we can find the true freedom that comes from doing God's will.

## Receptivity

There is in us as human beings a potent receptivity; a receptivity for which the word passivity is not accurate, though it has often been used for feminine receptivity. We have to find ways in which our will learns to work together with the will of God, as Mary did at the Annunciation.

It requires of us a receptivity to the Presence of God and what he asks of us. It may have to come via the earthy sanity of doubt: 'How shall this be, since I know not a man?' I sometimes find when I am talking with women who are very much against men, perhaps because of an abusive history, that we have to become aware that there is a way in which as women we have to find our sexual receptivity which is equal in its potency to the phallic power of penetration of the male. That receptivity belongs to the capacity to receive God. The Other may seem strange to us, almost overwhelming, but we have to find our receptivity so that we can meet with the other and be totally available: to be able to put ourselves at the disposal of the other. Our egotism, our self-obsession, our self-protectiveness goes deep. We have to find the place of choice: our sovereign freedom to say 'Yes' to God. That choice is his gift to us with all its terrors. The eventual 'Yes' may carry the creative 'No' of the ascetic path, or the questioning of our doubts. In order for Christ to be born again and again in the human spirit, not yesterday, not tomorrow but *now*, we have to find our way to receptivity and choice so that we can say our 'Let it be so.' The whole of our faith hung on that response at the Annunciation. More than we may ever know may hang on our response, too. That is why we offer ourselves through the Mother of God who discovered the place of ultimate choice. We need to find a listening, receptive obedience to God.

T. S. Eliot in *Four Quartets* points out that there is not only the one annunciation, but a 'lifetime of annunciations'. We meet each one and have to make something of what has come, however strange and alien it may seem at first—painful decision by painful decision sometimes. In the end, the annunciation we have to take on is death: how to give birth to the fact of one's own death? As Eliot said, 'The bone's prayer to Death its God. Only the hardly, barely prayable / Prayer of the one Annunciation.'[10] Sometimes, life's refusals of what we most desire (a partner, a child, an ambition...) has also to be accepted and taken in, so that we can find the otherness of the will of God for us.

---

[10] T. S. Eliot, *Collected Poems 1909–1962* (London: Faber & Faber, 1964), 208.

Yet, annunciations can bring rejoicings, too. We hear in the Gospel Mary went to her cousin Elizabeth in the hill country, Elizabeth said, 'As soon as the sound of your greeting reached my ears the baby in my womb leapt for joy' (Luke 1:44). Out of that meeting of the two women comes the great song of the Magnificat, held between them. It celebrates surely the Unexpected Joy (another of the liturgical and iconic titles of the Mother of God). 'From now on all generations will call me blessed. The Mighty One has done great things for me and holy is his Name.' It is a strange song, too: that great song of reversals. 'He has scattered the proud in their innermost thoughts. He has brought down the mighty but has lifted up the humble' (Luke 1:51). No pious passivity is noticeable there. I respond to the way Mary is inspiringly active and courageous. She is like David's wife-to-be, Abigail, who saddled up her ass and set out into the wilderness, or the Shunamite woman who did the same. The Mother of God could, too, as it were, saddle up her donkey and set out for the hill country, or Bethlehem, or Egypt, or Jerusalem—risking the journey into the wilderness of God, dependent on the mysterious divine guidance as the meaning of what was happening to her unfolded. She too was a travelling woman, who can travel with searching women today.

So, discovering the Virgin in experience can be joyful and celebratory as well as a massive risk, an offering that can be sacrifice—a total offering of self to the givenness of God. Virginity can be fecund, fruitful. It carries within it the fruitful womb. So Mary is not only Virgin, but Virgin Mother.

The Bible has many stories in it of children of promise who were born to barren women, way beyond the restraints of biology. The child of promise may be an actual child or may be the birth of the new in many forms. Even in periods of terrible spiritual sterility and barrenness, the Word of God still comes asking to be born in us.

> Sing, O barren one who did not bear; burst into song and shout, you who have not been in labour! For the children of the desolate woman will be more than the children of her that is married. (Is. 54:1)

The true meaning of the Gospel is full of these songs of reversal, of mind-splitting and heart-warming paradoxes and oxymorons, whose meanings only unfold through participation in life, and the life of faith.

## *Physicality*

There are spiritual meanings to the biological fact of womb. Phyllis Trible, in her book *God and the Rhetoric of Sexuality*, links the Hebrew word for womb with the one meaning tender, loving compassion.[11] Certainly in a life of faith we need to find the spiritual meanings that the womb engenders — and of which women may be the guardians but not the possessors of experience that belongs to the truly human. The spiritual womb can help us to bear, to carry, to gestate, to suffer things in order to wait for the right time for something to come to birth; equally to be able also to bear with the miscarriages, the abortions, the stillbirths that happen in all the situations which life in its raw, its fallen state, has to endure. How are we to become in the Church 'mothers-and fathers-in-Israel' for each other, in the company of the Mother of God and her great, varied and even morally questionable ancestresses? How can we learn spiritually to nurture, feed, train, give each other enough but not too much, without smothering each other with parasitic love which does not allow enough relational space for the other to become who they are? Sometimes the pains and sufferings involved will take us into having to learn from God what is told to us in Isaiah 45:3: 'I will give you the treasures of darkness, riches stored in secret places...' Dark times may be where the Lord most is:

> without darkness
> Nothing comes to birth,
> As without light,
> Nothing flowers.[12]

---

[11] Phyllis Trible, *God and the Rhetoric of Sexuality*, Overtures to Biblical Theology 2 (Philadephia: Fortress Press, 1978).

[12] May Sarton, *Collected Poems, 1930–1993* (W. W. Norton and Co., 1993), 326.

In the Mother of God, we have the one who could make something of the dark times. She was the one who learned to take the hard sayings and 'treasure them in her heart', able to do that which tests us all—how to endure not just our own suffering but the suffering of the Beloved. Mary found a way that kept her nailed to the foot of the Cross, when that was what was happening.

## Testing

Times of testing can make us feel very alone. The only icons in which Mary appears to be alone she is not truly so. For in reality the Mother of God Orans (the praying Mary) is joined with us and with her Son in his ever living to make intercession for us. Other than with her, as representing our offering to God in total self-givenness, so that he might come again and again and be incarnate in the human heart, where could we wish to be? To be with her as representing the ongoing life of the Church to worship and to pray for the sins and darkness of the world, which God loves—how could we settle for doing otherwise? Other than with her, essentially there is no other place where we as women and men in the Church can stand. She shows us the courageous and even daunting journey that has to be made. The 'feminine matrix' that her feasts give in liturgical form in the Orthodox tradition is a deeply satisfying resource for women in the Orthodox Church as it is for men. There may have to be transformations in the cultural application of some of the images, but the Presence of the Mother of God transcends them all with her 'Protecting Veil' that encompasses us all.

To sum up, I quote from Saint Silouan: his vision of the Mother of God. I first heard this passage read in an illuminating talk given by Bishop Kallistos:

> We cannot fathom the depth of the love of the Mother of God, but this, we know: The greater the love, the greater the suffering of the soul. The fuller the love, the fuller the knowledge of God. The more ardent the love, the more fervent the prayer. The more perfect the

love, the holier the life. […] The greater the love, the greater the sorrow. Never by a single thought did the Mother of God sin, nor did she ever lose grace, yet vast were her sorrows. When she stood by the Cross her grief was as boundless as the ocean and her soul knew pain incomparably deeper than Adam's suffering when he was driven from Paradise, for the reason that the measure of her love was beyond compare greater than the love with which Adam loved when he was in Paradise. […] We cannot discern to the full the love of the Mother of God, and so we cannot comprehend all her grief. Her love was complete. She stands in our midst as the one who calls us to give ourselves totally to God.[13]

---

[13] Archimandrite Sophrony (Sakharov), *Wisdom from Mount Athos* (London: DLT, 1973), 56–7.

# ANGER

## NOTE

This paper was delivered as a retreat address to the Sisters of the Love of God, Convent of the Incarnation, Fairacres, Oxford in March 1988. There was a discussion following the paper that allowed Wendy to expand on what she had said in the talk, which is included here.

## *Introduction*

Anger is quite a difficult subject and to encourage me I like to wear my Celtic brooch, which is, I think, the Dragon of Anger. In the Celtic tradition anger is an energy bound into the service of love.

I want to try to talk *gently* about the subject, because I think it is an extremely difficult one, and there is a tremendous weight of tradition behind all that we are trying to understand and explore in new ways. But I also want to speak not only gently, and in an exploring way, but also fairly *firmly*, for various reasons. Let me share some of those with you to begin with.

One is that as you know I spend a lot of my time listening to people where there are problems. I know just how many hours of that time is spent trying to help people to look at the things which are making them angry and that are buried very deep down, and finding that they cannot release their creative energies to love more deeply, more adequately, until some of this stuff has been brought out into the open, looked at, worked at, understood and in God's mercy transformed, quite often into a different kind of energy. In particular, I spend a good deal of my time listening to women who often have a particular problem about feeling that they should get their anger into the open. We have been brought up traditionally to feel that 'good, kind, nice, clean

Christian girls' do not do that sort of thing. Therefore, we feel very bad about it when it starts seeping out at the edges somewhere and catching up on us. Often that means that as women we get shut into a victim mentality, feeling badly done to—things always happening to us—but never quite being able to get them out and be worked upon because we will not look at the anger which is inside us about some of the things that have happened. So that we try, and I think this is one of the dangers of the contemplative life, to *absorb* the anger and the pain; at best leaving it open to Christ, to God, to do the absorbing, ultimately, for us, but in the process doing a great deal of absorbing somewhere in ourselves. So that what can happen is that we become like over-absorbent sponges: unwrung, flabby, full of the weight of stuff that we no longer know how to wring out in order to get some fresh approach to mopping up life again. We are left with the problem—how do we wring out the sponge which is us? And how do we get some of the creative energies of God moving in us and through us, to help in the process?

Then I do spend a great deal of my time listening to people from religious communities, not only Anglican but also Roman Catholic ones, where again and again some kind of picture unfolds often of aspects of community life being vitiated by long-standing unfinished business in human relationships where so much that has been going wrong has not been able to be brought out into the open for fear that it would bring too much bad feeling with it, too much initial anger. So that often in communities there are areas, pockets of 'bad' silence (and contemplative silence has its shadow side, hasn't it?)—silence can go bad on us at times so that often people are feeling appallingly miserable and wretched because something needs to get out into the open and be explored. Ninety-nine times out of a hundred when it is brought into the open there is a case to be heard, there is something going on that is wrong that could, under God's mercy, with a bit of hard work in human relationships, be sorted out; but we are sometimes afraid to get into it. It all turns claustrophobic; people become over-particular, hard on each other about what is going on, and try to deal with it by what I would call the 'repressive inspirational method', that is, you hold down the bad and you inspire people to be good. That is okay while the inspiring to be good lasts, but the bad is still held there somewhere, not really transformed and is liable to bubble out, seep out, explode out in banging doors and the exchange of 'notes' when diplomatic relationships have badly broken down. All those problems occasionally come, not only to me but to colleagues in my profession. Some of my colleagues are not Christian and will say 'there is so much anger in Christian Religious Communities, what is it all about? Why can't they deal with it? Why can't they be honest about it and work on it?'

And of course we are all trying to deal with our fear in our social and political life, the fear of what human anger and destructiveness faces us with in international relations, in our fear of The Bomb and so on. And we're all trying to look in every way we possibly can at what it means to make peace. Is there a making of peace which does involve a working with a process, a way, a taking-on-board the things which make for difference between human beings and finding a way to work with them, rather than just repress them and keep them under in an unstable state? Many Christians are able to talk more these days about the possibility of being angry with God, but I think that sometimes, for some of us, that can be a cop-out; that we can, as it were, fling stuff at God which we are not prepared to look at with each other and the problem can still go on in some mysterious way.

Now I do believe that prayer is essential. The Bible and tradition are divided on what we do with passions like anger. If we look, for instance, at the Epistle of James, it says, 'Everyone should be quick to listen, slow to speak and slow to become angry, because human anger does not produce the righteousness that God desires.' (Jas 1:19–20 NIV) And then on the other hand we turn to Ephesians and it says, 'putting away falsehood, let all of us speak the truth to our neighbours, for we are members one of another. Be angry but do not sin, do not let the sun go down on your anger.' (Eph. 4:25–6) Equally the tradition of the Church from the oldest time until now is divided and I know some of you have been sharing Bishop Kallistos's talks to the Community where he has been pointing out in the tradition that some Fathers of the Church would say 'mortify the passions', put to death things like anger; while others say, transform them, get hold of them, use them in the service of love. And it is in that latter tradition that in my profession I feel I have to stand. I have been greatly helped by Martin Buber's teaching on evil, and his teaching about how the evil impulse should be bound to its root in the service of God, which, I believe, is what the Celtic, tradition also stands for.

Alastair Campbell's book *The Gospel of Anger* is a superb book about anger, not only human anger but also about the anger of God.[1] Let me just read you a verse of Blake's before I pass on. He says:

> I was angry with my friend:
> I told my wrath, my wrath did end.
> I was angry with my foe,
> I told it not, my wrath did grow.[2]

It is the way untold, unworked-on anger becomes the 'wrath that grows'. I will not talk now about the anger of God, though there are things that could be said, but if you want to look at a particularly neat summary about what some of the ideas of the anger of God might be about in theological understanding, do look at Alastair Campbell's book.

What I think we need to do so urgently when we are looking at our anger is somehow to try to sever the link between anger and destructiveness and to realize that we *can* sever that link and do something with the space in between. Some of you may come from families and backgrounds where you have had such desperate experiences of people's anger that you know perfectly well that part of your search in the Religious Life is to do something about that and not to make other people suffer in the way you have suffered from excess anger. If we are talking about sharing anger obviously we are not talking about setting

[1] Alastair Campbell, *The Gospel of Anger* (London: SPCK, 1986).

[2] William Blake, 'A Poison Tree', from *Songs of Experience* (1794), in *Poetry and Prose of William Blake*, ed. Geoffrey Keynes (London: The Nonesuch Press, 1946), 76.

out to destroy each other through anger, which can happen; the bomb stands as a collective sign of that fact. But what we need to do is to get hold of our angry feelings and to realize that there can be a distance between feeling something, reflecting on it and recognizing it; thinking about it; deciding whether to let its energies out in the expression of emotion into action. In other words, often we can work on anger and find that there are stopping places. Sometimes to become aware of our anger, and know that is what I am feeling, and to ask, 'what can I do about it?' is enough to stop the boiling, surging part of it, and to enable us to reflect on where we can put some of it. Sometimes some of it can then be expressed, sometimes not. Equally I think there are times when we just have to be patient with each other: expressing anger explosively often clears the air quite remarkably (not always, but quite often). So we have to make space and time with ourselves and each other, with God in prayer and in relationships and in conversation and communication with others, where we are prepared to look at and work on some of the causes and after-effects. We have not too quickly to attempt to apologize when we have been angry or when we feel angry, trying to put the relationship right, before the issues of truth and justice and mercy have been worked through; because that is often what the issues are about. About things needing to be put right between people. I am wanting us to reflect on the possibility of acknowledging, identifying, understanding and communicating something about some of our angry feelings, because if we manage to get out some of that side of our feeling life, we then find that there are other drives present in the human being, by God's mercy, and one is a strong desire to make reparation. At times we may feel angry enough to want to destroy but equally there's a drive in me to repair, to put things right, to come back into relationship of love, to make amends, to reconcile. This is a real energy which is at work in human beings. But our reparative energy is only uncovered when our fears of anger and destructiveness have been really owned, and the anger underneath owned up to in some way. Many of us hold off from finding that we have this reparative zeal at work in us, which is the work of the Spirit

I believe, because we will not let ourselves get to the place where it dwells, because we have blocked up and dammed all that in a refusing to work through some of the difficulties.

I want to dispel two fallacies. One is the fallacy that to let off steam is in itself a good thing. There is a great deal of theory around saying that to vent anger is a good thing. Now sometimes it is good, just simply to do that—to let it out and then to calm down, to come back on the situation and talk about what can be done about it. But always to go round letting off steam on every conceivable occasion can become addictive and like any other addiction it's a bad thing when it gets to that stage. In other words, reflection, the exercise of good self-control, in moderation, is obviously important as well. Sometimes we need to let off steam, sometimes we *do not* need to let off steam, and we need to decide which. We can get addicted to being angry about things and there may be other things we can do more creatively instead. So that's one fallacy: not always to let off steam, but sometimes to allow it to happen and deal with it, Mop up the mess and deal with the underlying issues.

Then the second fallacy is the 'bottle it up for God' one. Somehow we think we are doing the right thing by God if we put anger down, repress it, bottle it up. We ignore the state of bodily arousal that anger brings and if we do that it often leads to negative withdrawal, to not caring about things. It erodes affection and trust between people. It sets up ulcers and the possibility of heart attacks and many other psycho-somatic things too. The part of it which is not transformed when it settles down somewhere underneath becomes hatred. I believe that hatred is bottled-up anger. Anger that is no longer an energy but is a still pool of negativity deep within the self. We need to do something to get at our hatred, our hostility, which can be passive, but very noticeable and very destructive of deep human relationships; to turn it through the energy of anger out into the open and into communication. Hatred appears at times in the form of rather cold character assassination, malice about others or emotional blackmail and is much harder to deal with in the end than anger ever is. We can nurse our anger, can't we, nourish it somewhere inside us, feed it on all the negative stuff?

In the end it can lead, in some people at least, to what Erich Fromm has called 'malignant anger'[3]—malignant, a sort of cancerous aggression which is not expressed but which is constantly at work in the personality; an anger which is cold rather than hot, that denies the human, that cuts off from association with others, that leads to a loss of social rootedness, any rootedness in community, in depth of relationship, and ends up as ennui (boredom), anomie (disregard of moral conventions), with the possibility of vandalism always underneath the surface, and in sadism. There is quite enough going around in our society that we now understand so much more about—sadism towards the weak, the vulnerable, children and animals—to make us take the possibility of building up malignant aggression seriously.

One of the problems about trying to share anger is surely the matter of timing. When is the right time to do it? It is difficult to find the right time sometimes, isn't it? Sometimes it explodes in an untimely way just when one least wants it to, and when there is not time to deal with it. There is also the fact that some people have a slow fuse and some people have a quick fuse, you know for some people the bit of blue paper is very short, you just put a match to it and it has gone up almost immediately, for other people there is a long piece of rope winding through the landscape and it can take years for it to reach the explosion point, but sooner or later it does. Equally there is a difference between people's cooling-off time afterwards. Some people can flare into anger and five minutes later can almost genuinely have forgotten all about it—the whole thing has gone and life has moved on. They

[3] [Erich Fromm first coined the term 'malignant narcissism' in 1964, describing it as a 'severe mental sickness' representing 'the quintessence of evil'. He characterized the condition as 'the most severe pathology and the root of the most vicious destructiveness and inhumanity'. It does not seem that Fromm ever used the term 'malignant anger'. However, Wendy is not alone in using this term (probably derived from her memory of Fromm): it was anticipated in Richard Watson, *Theological Institutes* (B. Waugh, and T. Mason, 1834), 392 (just a very passing comment, and unlikely to have reached Wendy), and also used in Dean Abbott, *Common Good: Reflections on Everyday Vices and Virtues* (Wipf and Stock, 2021), chapters 6 and 9. Ed.]

cannot understand it when someone is going round feeling hurt or upset because they've almost forgotten it ever happened. Other people can take three days, three weeks, three months, three years, three decades to get angry or to get over somebody's angry outburst with them. So we do have a real problem, don't we, about timing? And I certainly want to acknowledge that. Living together in community we have to know a great deal about each other's timing on matters of anger and on matters of forgiveness afterwards.

I want to try to share with you something about how we can learn to understand and recognize anger when we find it in ourselves and where the contemplative life and prayer has something specific to offer about that.

## The Importance of Anger

Why is anger important, why is it an important human experience, why is it there at all? First of all I think it helps over *separation*. We all know the tender, loving feelings that draw us together, towards other people, which can help us to identify with others, help us to participate with and in them, feel with them, unite with them, and obviously, that can take us into the depths of sexuality too. But equally we all have a need to be ourselves, to be who we are, to be separate from the other, and sometimes it is the energies which are to do with, differences, with a feeling of anger because one is so different from the other that can, as, it were, push people apart into being who they are, separate and independent. And if they can do that with clarity and know their own place, separate from the other then they can come together in relationship more effectively. Some relationships are in a terrible mess because everything is fused and mixed up together in the middle and people are not really apart at all and everything goes round and round in too small a claustrophobic system. It is only when you help people to push each other apart and find the internal space in the relationship that something can begin to change. It is often anger initially that provides the space. If I am really over against you, there is a chance that I can take you more seriously, that I can listen to you and not just feel intolerably fused and confused, so mingled with you. Confusion, when things have gone wrong in a relationship, has to become conflict, if it is to be sorted. Confusion doesn't change unless you meet the elements in the confusion expressed in conflict terms. So anger helps us to separate from each other and to find out something about our boundaries: what is you, what is me; where do you stop and I begin. It can help us to discover and make use of personal boundaries so that we don't invade each other in a negative way all the time.

Secondly, as I have already mentioned, it can bring clarity, a clearing of air which has become very foetid, tight, claustrophobic; a clearing of the air by owning up to our differences. It is often noticeable that we like, as women, to explore things through likenesses and sameness and being with each other; we find it less easy to be over against someone and look at differences. Anger is one of the things which expresses the fact that I am different, and that I need to speak from that place of difference sometimes.

I will just mention quickly too that it can be a release of repressed energy, the arousal of vitality and feeling after an illness; if there has been a profound introversion to an inward place, then anger can be that state of convalescence where vitality and energy are returning. I think we all know the times when we are impossible to handle when we are just recovering from something.

Let me just mention the more social aspect that anger is there in order to recognize and to right wrong, and to overcome injustice. Only with a certain degree of the conviction of knowing that a thing is wrong and that we cannot stand it any longer, either on one's own behalf or on behalf of others, can we really do something about it. Anger can help us to push for truth, it can give us the energy to challenge and change; it can be a goad against our complacency, our acceptance of things too easily. There's quite a bit in Alastair Campbell's book on that last point, just as there has been so much in the liberation theology in South and Central America which is about people who have been intolerably victimized for so long who, through anger initially, have found their energy to work to change things, and to work for justice and mercy in their society.

So those are some of the uses of anger, that is why we need to learn to use it creatively, it has its uses. Let us look now at how we can understand something about our own anger. By anger I mean *assertion*, the courage to be, the courage to be different from each other. Let's notice first of all that anger can take a number of different directions. It can move outwards towards other, in the form of anger, or rage, or wrath, or even at worst, paranoia—those are deepening stages. Paranoia is when we feel angry with the whole world because it appears to be totally against us. But equally anger can move inwards and turn against the self, and then it becomes depression, apathy, self-torture. Or it can get uneasily stuck half-way, neither in nor out, leaking out a bit in the form of irritation, misery, bad moods, sulks which are perfectly noticeable to other people, but aren't really coming out into the open and saying what they are, owning that there are angry feelings underneath, Also we can get anger denied, just not allowed to be there by consciousness. So that someone will come to us and say, 'I'm not angry, whatever makes you say I'm angry, of course I'm not angry, I'm never angry in my life, anger is one of the things I really feel I don't experience at all.'

## Using Anger to Hide other Feelings

I want to talk about how we can use anger to hide other feelings, as a defence. I want to take anger through. a number of stages. We can use anger as a defence against other feelings, and this is one of the interesting and exciting things about learning to work with the emotional life. You learn how one emotion moves into another, how one masks another and it is only when you get behind the mask of one that you find the other. So let's look at how we can use anger as a *defence*, to hide other things.

First of all we can use it as a defence to hide *fear*—a sort of angry bravado about life; we go around pretending, oh yes, we can cope, and being pretty courageous, a bit pushy and angry, but underneath we're quaking a bit, quailing a bit, just being angry to hide our fear. So that we not only need someone to acknowledge our anger with us, but also to say, 'It's a bit shaky, you know, is there something behind it?' to try and help us to get at what lies behind it—the fear. Can you think of situations where you have experienced that? We have put up a good show and been fairly assertive and angry, but underneath we have been feeing something else.

Then there is something men quite often talk about, the way in which they feel they use a rather angry, assertive, upfront approach to life, to hide their fear of tenderness, to mask their *tenderness* because they have a fear of intimacy which makes them vulnerable. They do not like the feeling of being vulnerable to others so that they tend to hide it behind an angry, assertive could not care less, macho, cowboy approach to life. Men tend to talk about this—but also some women. Certainly in Oxford I have met some women academics who are often leading rather lonely, isolated lives from the feeling point of view. They have found that they feel much too vulnerable about their unlived-out tenderness and that if they get anywhere near it they might weep. They do not want to do that, so they hide it under a fairly intellectually assertive approach to life—pushing the young students not to be so stupid about feelings, to get on and do some hard work—that kind of approach.

Equally if we are feeling bad about something, if we are feeling *guilt*, we can use anger to cover up the fact that we know we are in the wrong somewhere. So we can get angry, pushing other people off when we know we are feeling bad about something, to hide the guilt.

Sometimes the young people will talk about the way they will hide the fact that they are attracted towards someone else, they feel desire towards someone; but they are a bit afraid of how they are going to handle it or manage it, so again they pass it off with an angry pushy approach to the other, turning them away putting them off and so on because they are afraid of the *attraction*, the pull towards the other that they're feeling. It is amazing how many of us are afraid of intimacy. I know it is particularly a deep fear in many men that if they come too close to someone they will lose their autonomy; they have a sense that there is something about the feeling life, something about women, about the feminine, which sucks them into a spiralling, floating vortex in which they feel rather caught and sticky and they do not know how to get out and fear they are losing their independence, so that many boys/men will certainly put up anger against feelings of attraction: towards others which threaten them with intimacy, with vulnerability. But equally girls too. If you watch groups of adolescents you see a lot of the playing around with the attraction theme, through putting off people, being assertive, pushing them away, but underneath you also feel they are saying 'come on'. That is a mix of feeling, isn't it?

Then after death or bereavement, part of the bereavement process is the way in which anger can hide our *grief*. We can be so desperately hurt by the death of someone we love that we become angry, as a way of defending ourselves against that sense of intolerable loss, the feeling that we have lost the other; but not only have we lost the other, we have lost ourselves in the process because so much of our being was bound up in the other. Sometimes the only way to hold off that sense of collapse and loss is to become angry about things, to fight about things, to fight the doctors or the nurses who looked after the people, or to fight the relatives over the will, or whatever it is. It can be so desperately destructive of course in families and in relationships, but we are covering up a deep sense of bereavement, grief, the experience of loss.

Then *inadequacy* and *insecurity*. This is a bit like the fear and bravado one: we can use anger to hide our inadequacy, our insecurity, to pretend that we are more capable of coping with life than we really are.

And then finally we can use anger to hide even more painful emotions like *envy*, our sense of lack, our sense of longing that things could be different; we do not admit that we are envious of someone, we just think that we are justifiably angry with them for some reason. But underneath we are really envious. That deep sense of lack, of longing, of poor self-image makes us envious of others and therefore angry with them. I read an article recently by Susie Orbach who works in the London Women's Therapy Centre and she was saying that in groups of women, where for so long they had been helping each other climb out of experiences of depression and inadequacy, they found that once they had really begun to come out of these states then they had to meet envy of each other which had a destructive effect on the progress of the group until it was properly owned up to and looked at. And indeed it is the reason why some people do not make it out of a depression, because the minute they begin to feel less depressed they then find that they are really envious of other people who are managing life better than they are, looking better, better dressed, better able to cope with their jobs. All kinds of things go on inside people, and they just feel 'I can't make the climb, I can't cope with the amount of bad feelings I have about others, now that I'm beginning to come out of my depression and look at my own self-image and what I can do with it.' So there is a very real, painful bit of work to be done somewhere, between anger, envy and a profound longing that life could be different, that one might find a better self-image, better sense of the self to live with.

We sometimes have to do a lot of work on ourselves in prayer before God, I think, trying to work out what our anger is doing. Is it hiding something else? That is one form of interior monasticism, an interior asceticism we have to go through; a differentiation, working out what things are about, deciding to do something with them. And then we also have to look at whether we are acknowledging anger at all. So let us turn it round now and look at it from the other side.

How can we use other things to mask the anger? We have been looking at using anger to hide other feelings, now what about other things hiding the anger? I am sorry to run through this in such a list but I hoped that if I left you with material, you might be able to think it through and work on it rather than me amplifying it too much tonight.

## The Masks of Anger

If someone wants to be angry but cannot be because they are afraid of the other person or because they feel they should not be angry, then it will leak out somewhere. And where it can come out is in things like, firstly, an *anxiety* to please. We all want to please each other generally, to get on with each other, but if we have got into a state where we are *anxious* to please, it often means that we are hiding negative feelings, and the anxiety is the way it is being expressed. Here we tend, when faced with a situation which could be a bit confrontational, where a bit of anger, assertiveness, courage-to-be might come into the open, to give up. We cannot say no, and we instead resort to whining, moaning, nagging and trying to make peace at any price, which has such dire effect on the truth in the long run.

Secondly, a continuation of the same thing, a general *compliance* and *conformity* in life, where there is a great desire, not to give up necessarily, but to give in, to fit in, to be a 'nice, kind, clean, good' Sister, or Oblate, or therapist, or whatever; to fit in, and that involves us in a denial of our shadow side, the dark side of ourselves. But we feel that we dare not show these other feelings because of a loss of our preferred self-image. I like people to think I am nice and kind and good and it is difficult for me to yield that, there is a lot of nice secondary gain that comes through that image. I get praise, I get worship, I get pats on the back if that is how I am, and we do not want to let other things through for fear we lose that. And we all the time need to look at what is called in my trade 'secondary gains'. Why do we go on with absolutely appalling behaviour? Because we are getting something out of it. And that is the nasty part to try and get hold of. What am I getting out of this, that makes me go on behaving in this stupid way? That is where we can catch ourselves and where we can feel such shame when we realize what it is we are doing like preserving a kind of self-image. When I talk at staff-support groups at Sobell House with the nurses there they will all say that the one image they cannot afford to lose is the image of the nurse as 'coper': you have got to cope, you have to be seen to cope and nothing on earth will make you do something like get angry or upset or say you have had enough, or you will not have any more, or saying 'no' to the constant push from the doctors about what they think you should do, because if you do they say, 'what is the matter with so-and-so—I have never seen her like that, I always thought, she could cope with anything.' This word 'cope'! Well, now; I am sure there are words that each of you have in your work or your family that you know you do not want to lose. But when that gets a hold on someone's life, a rather cringing, self-hating mould forms underneath. You hate yourself because you know you are conforming, you are not really being yourself—and you're not really being truthful about situations: you despise yourself so that it tends to lead into that regressive inward spiral towards depression.

Equally *clinging* can hide anger, or very negative feelings of various kinds, because it is an anxious dependency, the kind of dependency where we need to hold on to something because we are so afraid that if the truth did come out we would be rejected. Often because we are hiding what we know could come out—namely, some of our angry feelings about the other—we get very anxious that the other will pick them up. Underneath that experience is often the way in which the person on whom we are dependent has been harbouring angry feelings about us and unacknowledged feelings of rejection. Mothers of young children often try to hide too much their desire to reject the child at times but the child picks it up underneath somewhere and knows that the parent is angry, and it is better for a child sometimes to face anger from a parent than to face the feeling that there is something wrong that is not being expressed so that it makes me cling to you and I do not know what it is about. That is much worse: it makes what has been called the 'double bind' problem. A double bind is when someone gives us two messages at the same time. They say, 'I love you, I love you, I love you (but I hate you so much that I wish you'd go away).' I will try and give you an example of this. I was on a bus coming from North Oxford the other day and there was a mother with a small child, and the small child was running round the top deck of the bus, a bit out of control, and the mother was saying, 'Melanie, Melanie come here, dear, come here darling, Melanie, Melanie come here.' And you could feel the tension mounting in the sweetness of her voice. Eventually the child drifted back along the aisle banging into everybody on the way, and as she got near the mother, the mother who had gone on using this sweet-sweet tone, took the child round the elbow so tightly and *plonked* her on her knee and you felt the child had been drawn by the sugary

Anger

tone and then suddenly met the 'plonk'. Well, that's the double bind—in a totally-understandable form. But you know what I mean: the kind mother that we all are when our children begin to leave home and we say, 'Yes, of course, darling, I want you to go, I want you to have your freedom, but the fact is I'll have a heart attack if you step over the threshold.' We give out contradictory messages so that the other becomes very resentful with the feeling of being unappreciated for the person who they genuinely are. Something is never quite straight. Now it is that kind of double bind communication that is often very noticeable indeed in the families where there is very disturbed behaviour: too much double-bind, too much hate—lurking under the appearance of love, without its reality.

And then a deep anger can hide itself under *generalized irritability*. And this is the half-in, half-out sort of thing. This is when we go, as they say, bitching about detail, never pleased, never satisfied, never suited. Adopting a sort of vigilante attitude towards others and never letting anything pass under our eye or pass our ear, or under our nose, always there, always noticing. A real angry attentiveness can hide itself under this rather generalized irritable approach. In communities where there is too much of that going on, there is always pettiness, feuding, backbiting and so on. Generalized irritability is both interior and exterior. We can be nagging away at ourselves and we can be nagging away at others—both—and we are hardly noticing what is inside and what is outside. It is the sort of state in which I get up in the morning in middle age I find—a generalized irritability, just feeling that you have got out on the wrong side, and then you go down to breakfast and start picking on everybody and they think, 'Heads down, Mum's here!' It is far better if one just had a brief private explosion about how furious one was at having to face the day and then get on with it, but instead one takes it out on everyone and everything including oneself.

And then a form that is quite difficult to come to terms with, or to do anything with. We can hide anger under *aggressive teasing*. Teasing other people in a fairly aggressive way which has a put-down effect. When the person complains they say, 'I was only teasing, can't you take

125

a joke? Haven't you got a sense of humour?' And what can you say in response to that, except feel a bit guilty and that perhaps it was a joke, and it can be very devastating to people, really undermining, and there is no answer to it because the anger is hidden.

We can hide our anger under *silence*, the withdrawal method of showing anger, where we can feel, and be, cold and cut off, and where we can use silence to manipulate other people because often we are denying our anger and pushing it all on to the other so that the other will be the one who explodes. How often I have heard this talked of in marriages where often the man retreats into silence, the woman explodes and then, she says, she feels childish, stupid, and she is accused of being emotional and he remains righteous and cold and calm, cool and collected and extremely powerful. Obviously this is one of the things that needs to be considered in living a contemplative life with the emphasis on silence—silence can be of many forms, there can be bad silences, and we can use them in a wrong way. We can even use the Christian withdrawal into prayer and absorption in such a way that others feel it as a threat because they are left doing all the messy stuff like showing anger and other messy feelings. A sulking, grudging approach to life too often hides behind the silence. The sulking which goes on for months before you know what's wrong, and the grudge which goes on for months afterwards because we won't forgive. All that can hide under a general, cold, silent, controlled powerfulness.

Then we can hide our anger under *displacement* masks where we can pass the anger down the pecking order, as it were; we cringe to the boss and we kick the cat, at the bottom of the pile. Now it is perfectly natural, all of us go in for displacement behaviour but sometimes it can be extremely unfair (for instance on the cat!) or on the child or the Novice or on the Oblate or whoever it is who catches it at the bottom of the pile. People who are being very compliant and anxious to please towards people at the top of the hierarchy can be unspeakable to someone who happens to be working with them in the kitchen, or the laundry or whatever. It can happen to all of us, can't it? It happens in the home, it happens in religious communities.

Now I have fed in a lot of things about ways in which anger can hide other things and ways in which we can hide our anger that gives us a great deal to reflect on in relation to our own personal stories about anger and where these things belong within our faith and within a community. What do we understand from that deep place of commitment to our faith? Are there ways in which we can get hold of some of this difficult stuff, share it with each other sometimes, work on the things which have made an unjust situation, an unfair situation; work to change them, work to get out some of the pent-up irritation, or some of the deep-seated cold hatred that may be building up? Are there ways in which we can help each other with this? Are there ways in which we really can open it in prayer to Christ so that the transforming powers of the love of God can work through us and in it? But let us not try to work on an understanding of prayer that makes us in the end inhuman, or that we're the ones who are thought to be doing the absorbing all the time.

I was talking to someone, if I may say so, who had recently talked about her to someone in a religious community and she said the other person was so terribly nice about it and kind and encouraged her to talk about it all, to explode it and so on. But she said that in the end she was left holding something about it because the other person had been so different from herself, been so kind and nice about it, that she felt all the bad stuff was on her side and all the good stuff was on the other side and there wasn't an exchange of energies. Now how can we get the right exchange of energies between people so that transformative energies are at work, where I am taking responsibility for my anger as well, even when I'm listening to another person who is bringing anger to me? We cannot just do it by trying to present the opposite to them because otherwise the thing stays split, we have to find a way of moving it backwards and forwards by being able to own it and talk through it, I think.

# DISCUSSION

QUESTION: I would like to ask you about absorption. Sometimes you absorb anger without realizing it and it catches up with you. You talked about trying to separate it, to defuse it, but I'm not quite sure how it happens.

WENDY: Yes, I think there are a number of things we have to learn to do. One is to try to let go and say, 'let go, let God'. I think it means that when we do have some space we have genuinely to try to turn round on the experiences we've had during the day and say, 'Wait a minute what was going on, what have I been absorbing, perhaps in the wrong way? Let me name it, let me put it into words.' Certainly sometimes in my room I stamp on the floor, pound on the chair a bit, and try and express the anger at least to myself, and that I consider is part of my prayer. I am saying this to God: 'I can't, I won't because it's not mine, it's yours somehow—or you can do it through me, but I can't do it.' But that only works if I really get hold of it and express it and put it out into the open. Sometimes I have to go and talk to a colleague and say, 'look I don't know what's the matter with me, I'm just carrying too much, can you listen to me for a bit and try and see which bits are catching me somewhere?' *I think we have to learn to use each other*. I mean with colleagues who are friends, I say, and they say to me occasionally, 'look I need a session!' which means 'I really want to talk through something, will you be a perceptive listener?' not: 'we are just going to chat as friends'. And I think to be able to say to each other occasionally, 'can I have a session with you, I'm just too pent up, I'm carrying too much, I need to offload a bit: can you listen to it, push it around a bit for me?' that often really does do quite a lot: it is like harrowing the land, it breaks up the clods a bit.

And then in the longer term, we just have to try to open all these things to God. I have been intensely aware during the last two or three years of Raphael being the angel of healing and I try continually to be aware of the presence in the room of the angel of healing as well as the presence of God, and to live with some sense of the 'between', and, instead of taking things into me, putting them 'between' me and the other, between me and the presences all around so that one doesn't work with too profound a sense of inwardness, but a sense of between-ness, a sense of sharedness. Again, that is part of one's praying about it, I think.

QUESTION: You talked about people who can sulk for weeks, and I wonder whether to try to clear the air, or create a space is the right thing to do with some people, because they are so hurt by anger and take it so badly. Perhaps you have to have two people of like mind who want to make reparation for whatever is wrong. What do you do if one does not want to?

WENDY: It is often a long drawn-out process to begin work on all the repressed. things that have built up between people, and in families. I think that is why so much of the recent work on the healing of the memories and healing of the family tree is important. We sometimes have to be involved in a long process of reflection and communication to see what really has been going on. But in the more immediate situations, if one does not look at the cause of one's anger it is such a waste of a good energy source, as Evagrius says, 'don't waste good anger!'

QUESTION: Do you think that all outbursts of anger are irrational to some extent?

WENDY: There are two ways of being rational. One is with the reasons of the mind, that can be spelt out in thought, thinking terms and so on, but I think there are reasons of, the heart which are about our feelings and the way they work which have a logic of their own if we learn to understand them. When we call something irrational, we usually mean it is to do with the feeling area, the heart stuff, rather than the head, thought. I think that nearly all our emotions have their own way of being rational if we can learn to understand them and work with them, but the processes involved are different from thinking with the head.

QUESTION: I think people often have very deep-seated feelings that they want to put things right and yet can't, and I think this is where we can hold things up to the healing of God.

WENDY: There is such a depth of stuff in some families which cannot be talked about because of the fear that someone's feelings will be hurt, or that he or she will not be able to bear the truth. But often people are longing to put things right on some deeper level and sometimes one needs to take risks, but to do it if possible, with prayer around it. I've had such good experiences of going to people with my anger and saying that I want to reflect on it, talk about it with the person, and I believe it can help to heal long standing situations. It requires a lot or courage, and you have to be reasonably sure that the other person will be able to respond enough to get the dialogue going, but it does seem worth far more risks than we usually take.

QUESTION: Some things (personal experiences) are so untalkable about, aren't they? that they have to go on into the next life unhealed, and one just has to surround that sort of thing with prayer.

WENDY: Is it not the experience of some of us that experiences we have had within the family, and which certainly could not be healed within the family, we have been able to explore with a God-friend, therapist or someone, in such a way that something has moved on considerably? I can remember when I was in therapy the moment came when I realized I had forgiven my father for dying when I was a baby that I had got past the point where I thought men would always die on one, not live to see one through. So sometimes a third-party exploration can help.

QUESTION: I think one should always pay much more attention to the results of the anger than the cause, though I know you have to understand the causes, and you must look both to control it and to be compassionate towards other people. I feel it is a very great danger that because one suffers a great deal in anger, and one

causes a lot of suffering one spends too long being almost indulgently analytical about the causes of the anger. It's the results that
matter, the damage caused.

WENDY: Of course, it can be true that one is too indulgently self-reflec-
tive. But it is surely connected to the point I raised from Alastair
Campbell about how one must break the link between anger and
destructiveness. You are quite right, it is the results of one's anger
that matter. It is no good me being so angry that I go and kill
someone, but it is how to try and break that link, to say, 'I'm
angry, I want to kill a person' (if I do at that moment), but why
am I angry, what can I do with it, can I take it to them in a different mode? That does not seem to me to be over-done reflection.
Certainly, I can think of states when I stew over my anger in some
form of grievance, when I am not really working on it—that
would be self-indulgent. I think there are ways of reflection, putting something back and forth between oneself and whatever is
causing, the anger that is creative.

QUESTION: Surely creative use of anger quite often happens after the explosion: one has to release something first?

WENDY: Yes: sometimes the anger comes just like that; something
triggers it, and we can become so cowardly that if someone has
exploded at us we just creep away and are glad that it is blown
over a bit and some kind of relationship is still there, and we tend
then to think that 'I am not going to go back and talk about it because; it might set her off again, I can't bear that.' So we never do
the reparative work of sorting out what the difficulties really were
about, and to work on the injustices that were concerned. One has
to keep getting the coward back up front, and say, 'look, it is important, something did happen, it is worth looking at.'

QUESTION: I do not think we have to take other people's anger on ourselves. One can say: I don't think that really has anything to do
with me, and I am not going to take it on.

WENDY: It is how to get rid of the guilt bit. One feels that in any anger
I must be guilty of something and it is how to see the guilt as a

self-indulgence too. Some of us are chronic guilt-inducers in others: if you make the other person feel bad, then you have won really, haven't you, by some devious means.

QUESTION: I found what you said about the various masks of anger helpful. I think most of us feel angry either because our preserves are being poached upon, or because we feel we are in some way being diminished. If one looks at it and asks, 'Why am I angry?', and sees the reason, one can say what a silly thing to be angry about.

WENDY: Yes indeed, I know that traditionally it was said that one should not be angry because it is only one's pride that is being hurt, but this somehow is not good enough. Alastair Campbell is saying that if we rule out the possibility of God's anger, if we refuse to see that one of the faces of love can be anger then we are liable to develop a doctrine that Christians should not be angry. But if we can allow that one of the faces through which love passes can be anger because of unfairness, injustice, differences, then we can allow that to ourselves. I think it is a terribly important point that if we make God too loving without any of the energies that come from things like anger then we have, as it were, to imitate that.

QUESTION: I was struck with what Wendy said about the deep reparatory zeal that there is in each of us, but that in order to tap into that we have to clear the angry feelings that are superimposed on it. I suppose it struck me because of all that Fr Cary wrote about reparation, and because of the struggles I have when I am angry myself.

WENDY: A woman called Barbara Dockar-Drysdale had a school for very disturbed children.[4] She described how they were all very angry indeed and very destructive, but how they would also, after an angry destructive bout, make some reparatory symbolic act asking to be received back, but you had to recognize what the symbolic act was. She said the way we usually deal with children's angry

---

[4] Barbara Dockar-Drysdale or Barbara Estelle Gordon (1912–1999) was a British psychotherapist who started the Mulberry Bush School for troubled children after the Second World War.

outbursts is to say, 'you have to say you're sorry', and the child learns to go through the formula of restoring relationships through these kinds of words, but it never meets its own heart, where it knows what it means to make reparation. And she says that our over quick polite form of dealing with things, like saying 'I'm sorry' and 'thank you', can mean that we are cut off from the real roots of things within us. If we have been angry we do feel guilty and our first instinct is to go and restore the relationship but sometimes it means that the other stuff doesn't get worked through. It is how to do both things, how to enable the relationship to go on but also to say 'I do want to talk about the differences between us'; we cannot just say, 'please forgive me, everything's gone wrong', and start with a clean slate. It's not as simple as that every time. A couple I worked with were talking about how. they had made a rule that they. would never let the sun go down on their wrath, and it was very good in some respects—at least they were on speaking terms—but they had also come to realize that as a result some of the deeper things never got worked through. It was as though they had to say, 'OK, but let's talk some of this through, tomorrow or at the weekend.' There had to be both things. I want to come back to the subject of guilt. I do feel that guilt is its own reward—it can be a great self-indulgence. Something goes wrong and a person says, 'I feel guilty, I feel guilty about it all'; and goes away and beats their breast. And people feel unconsciously that they have done enough by feeling guilty, so they do damn all about setting out to improve the behaviour, the guilt has been enough. It is almost as though we have to give up the guilt thing and look at the relationship and what needs altering.

QUESTION: You (and others) are saying that it is important to go and talk things through. I can never find the words to do that, and that, in itself, makes me angry... working things out over a long period of time seems to demand a communication skill most people don't have and maybe that's why they take out their anger in a physical way.

WENDY: There are many more ways of communicating than through words, violent and non-violent: someone makes a symbolic gesture, they suddenly put an arm round you when they are passing and you know that they are saying a great deal through that.

QUESTION: Do you not also need words? Is there not an ultimate need to put things into words, to clarify for yourself if nothing else?

WENDY: Sometimes, that is why it can be nice to work with someone who will quietly talk a little bit, and a little bit another time, and try it out as it were.

QUESTION: The trouble is your mind has to work at quite a fast pace to formulate the words; very often your emotions are going at a much faster rate.

WENDY: My godmother has M.S. and is in a wheel chair and in talking to me of her experience she says that it is almost as though, as the body found it more difficult to manoeuvre itself, she came to feel that language was like a body, and *that* 'body' went to pieces just as she felt her physical body was going to pieces so that over the years she says what you do, as the experience (of anger and frustration) becomes too big for words. You have to learn patience with the body of language as well as with the physical body.

QUESTION: Is it a question of temperament, not just the circumstances? But you change with your circumstances.

WENDY: Both are true. It all sounds so easy to talk about putting one's feelings into words, but it isn't. To name one's feelings is not easy.

QUESTION: One of the difficulties of a community situation is that we cannot express either anger or friendship except in words—or we can, but it is difficult. But we have these same strong feelings, either anger or love. I was thinking about the phrase 'a good anger'; again, in community if someone is angry it is a kind of tribute in that the person is noticing who you are and coming forth as who she is even if the circumstances seem rather bizarre.

QUESTION: I was talking with someone yesterday about prayer as relationship with God and how it embraces all one's everyday life and relationships, so that one's anger towards other people is entirely relevant to one's relationship with God. But I have been wondering about the question which originated all this: what is the place of anger in the contemplative life?

QUESTION: Fr Gilbert used to say that we were all meant to be reconcilers, to bring good out of situations which could be potentially bad, and I think this is what we should try to do, in very small ways, not necessarily dramatic. Whatever comes to hand we should try to use as a sort of reconciling power and bring God into it. Where things are very painful I think we just have to hold them within ourselves and trust to the healing power of God, whether we feel we are doing something or not.

WENDY: In a way that is consenting to be the third party in a situation. Having been a Quaker I know some of the Quakers who have been involved in big peace-keeping negotiations. They learnt to stand in the middle and allow a difficult situation to become a worse conflict for a while because it is necessary to sort out the confusions into what the conflict is really all about and to stay in the middle and attempt to keep people talking to each other. You cannot do that if you are just a sponge, you cannot just do it through absorbing, you have also got to take quite a firm peace-making line; sometimes it is through listening and some-times it is through trying to point out differences and contradictions—it is a real art. I love that verse about 'God was in Christ reconciling the world to himself' because I feel that somehow in Christ God was helping us to forgive him for the way the world is, because there is such pain. and such wicked-ness, and such cruelty and destructiveness that even if it is there because God gave us the gift of creative freedom, and we make all the wrong choices, nevertheless it is the Job situation and some of it is incommensurable. We cannot understand it and yet somewhere God was saying something in Christ about himself. It is a two-way reconciliation.

QUESTION: What do you do when you realize people envy you because you do not have their misfortunes and problems?

WENDY: Some of the women's groups have been forced into exploring envy because they found that once those who had been so downtrodden had begun to come out and fight and be more powerful about their own lives, they then began to envy each other much more. But often they found that what was important about the envy was not its destructive powers, though it certainly had that, but that it was also expressing some tremendous longing deep inside to realize one's own gifts, one's own talents, to develop oneself in some way; and they said that if they could get it back off its destructiveness into what it is one is really longing for, what is it that's so unfulfilled in one, how one can find some talent that one can use or develop, it often changed. That is interesting, isn't it? as a creative way of getting hold of one's envy. We never admit, you cannot usually get people to admit, to envy. We do not like to admit we feel that about other people—it is a mean thing to do. If you have come to feel like a sponge which is too full, what for you wrings the sponge, especially in prayer, in one's relationship to God? Is there some way in getting the sponge acted on, through prayer as well as through other ways?

QUESTION: I suppose really it is letting go, letting God take it instead of you. Fr Gilbert told me once when I had been praying for somebody, 'Oh, you've been doing it all wrong' and so I asked how. He said that I had been making the effort and lifting the person up to God (which is how I think I had been taught to do it) but that prayer is like a triangle: you have God at the top, you have yourself and the person that you are praying for. And he said if you go to the person and lift them up to God you are doing it the wrong way—what you must do is go to God and get him to come down to the person. That stops you from feeling it is all your hard work. So if you are beginning to feel like a sponge because everyone is loading things on to you can say to God, 'Come down and take this sponge away.' Perhaps this is the way to think about it.

WENDY: Yes, we need to learn a lot about the letting-go process: what do we mean, how do we do it, what does the triangle feel like, how do we activate it?

QUESTION: How do you know whether you have let something go—particularly something long-standing?

WENDY: Do you think you know when it has really happened? For instance, when forgiveness has really happened there is a sense of lightness—almost a physical thing, and so with letting-go.

QUESTION: To do that you have to be aware you are carrying it in the first place.

WENDY: Sometimes the image of 'the between' (it is from Martin Buber) helps me. When you and I meet there is a 'between' which forms itself if the relationship works. So that what happens is not a possession or your possession, it is something we participate in and share. And if I can believe that the other person's illness or problems (or whatever it is) is in the between, so that I do not have to take it all into myself, so that I hold it between me and the other person, and know that God is forming the between and is the presence in the between, then I may not get into the position of taking too much into myself anyway.

QUESTION: There is one translation of that verse 'the kingdom of heaven is between you'.

WENDY: Yes, sure, and the Holy Spirit as the 'go-between-God', in John Taylor's phrase. So that it is triadic but one need not think of a triangle with God always 'up there'.

QUESTION: I find it helps just to say, 'I am feeling like this' (whatever it is) and to hold my feelings, not repress them, just hold them—something happens, changes.

WENDY: Someone I was talking to the other day was talking about just that. She was a person who suffers a great deal from panic, and she had had a dream. She was sitting holding a black ball in her hands and that felt all right and then she leaned down to see what it was, and all sorts of gases started escaping from the ball and she felt completely overwhelmed and panicky and lost. As we were talking about it, she said she began to realize more what her panic was about, and that she was able in a sense to hold it, but what she must not do was lean her head into it so that she was getting the gases. She must learn to hold it; and perhaps even to put it down at a distance instead of having to hold it all the time.

QUESTION: I think it is sometimes difficult to be perfectly honest about how we do feel because we would think we are such horrible people, we would think it was the bitter end.

WENDY: It is a contradiction, isn't it—that we are taught it is right to be the sinner and yet as a Christian one should be 'good'. It is the difficult business of trying to live a moral life as a Christian and still collapse it back into penitence and say, 'I am a sinner, Lord have mercy'.

I would like to end with a poem by George Herbert which describes both sides of this dilemma:[5]

> Ah my deare angrie Lord,
> Since thou dost love, yet strike;
> Cast down, yet help afford;
> Sure I will do the like.
> I will complain, yet praise;
> I will bewail, approve:
> And all my sowre-sweet dayes
> I will lament, and love.

---

[5] George Herbert, 'Bitter-sweet', in *The Works of George Herbert*, ed. F. E. Hutchinson (Oxford: Clarendon Press, 1941), 171.

# SLG PRESS PUBLICATIONS

www.slgpress.co.uk